China's Rise in Africa

In seeking to cultivate external relations with African countries, China has long stressed its commonly shared roots with African nations as a developing country rather than a Western state, and as such the symbolic attraction of China clearly reverberates with many African elites who seem to look on China as a positive development model. However, it should be noted that this has not been embraced solely by dictatorial or authoritarian regimes but in fact China's approach to non-interference has struck a chord even with those democratically elected leaders in Africa. While such practices clearly benefit African elites, it remains doubtful that they do so for ordinary Africans, although sustained analysis suggests that potential exists, albeit hampered by the modalities of governance on the continent.

This book brings together experts on the topic to throw light on some of the more contentious aspects of the relationship.

This book was published as a special issue of the *Journal of Contemporary African Studies*.

Dominik Kopiński is Assistant Professor at the Institute of International Studies, University of Wrocław, Poland.

Andrzej Polus is Assistant Professor at the Institute of International Studies, University of Wrocław, Poland.

Ian Taylor is Professor at the University of St Andrews and University of Stellenbosch.

China's Rise in Africa
Perspectives on a Developing Connection

Edited by
Dominik Kopiński, Andrzej Polus and Ian Taylor

LONDON AND NEW YORK

First published 2012
by Routledge
2 Park Square, Milton Park, Abingdon, Oxon, OX14 4RN

Simultaneously published in the USA and Canada
by Routledge
711 Third Avenue, New York, NY 10017

First issued in paperback 2013

Routledge is an imprint of the Taylor & Francis Group, an informa business

© 2012 The Institute of Social and Economic Research

This book is a reproduction of the *Journal of Contemporary African Studies*, vol. 29, issue 2. The Publisher requests to those authors who may be citing this book to state, also, the bibliographical details of the special issue on which the book was based.

All rights reserved. No part of this book may be reprinted or reproduced or utilised in any form or by any electronic, mechanical, or other means, now known or hereafter invented, including photocopying and recording, or in any information storage or retrieval system, without permission in writing from the publishers.

Trademark notice: Product or corporate names may be trademarks or registered trademarks, and are used only for identification and explanation without intent to infringe.

British Library Cataloguing in Publication Data
A catalogue record for this book is available from the British Library

ISBN13: 978-0-415-68887-1
ISBN13: 978-0-415-84648-6

Typeset in Times New Roman
by Taylor & Francis Books

Disclaimer
The publisher would like to make readers aware that the chapters in this book are referred to as articles as they had been in the special issue. The publisher accepts responsibility for any inconsistencies that may have arisen in the course of preparing this volume for print.

Contents

1. Contextualising Chinese engagement in Africa
   Dominik Kopiński, Andrzej Polus and Ian Taylor — 1

2. From refusal to engagement: Chinese contributions to peacekeeping in Africa
   Wu Zhengyu and Ian Taylor — 9

3. The 'voracious dragon', the 'scramble' and the 'honey pot': Conceptions of conflict over Africa's natural resources
   Péter Marton and Tamás Matura — 27

4. Uneasy allies: China's evolving relations with Angola
   Lucy Corkin — 41

5. Sino-Zambian relations: 'An all-weather friendship' weathering the storm
   Dominik Kopiński and Andrzej Polus — 53

6. Sino-Indian co-operation in Africa: Joint efforts in the oil sector
   Karolina Wysoczańska — 65

7. The European Union and China's rise in Africa: Competing visions, external coherence and trilateral cooperation
   Maurizio Carbone — 75

8. China's 'soft power' in Africa?
   Łukasz Fijałkowski — 95

Index — 105

Contextualising Chinese engagement in Africa

Dominik Kopiński, Andrzej Polus and Ian Taylor

University of Wrocław and University of St Andrews/University of Stellenbosch

> In seeking to cultivate external relations with African countries, China has long stressed its commonly shared roots with African nations as a developing country rather than a Western state, and as such the symbolic attraction of China clearly reverberates with many African elites who seem to look on China as a positive development model. However, it should be noted that this has not been embraced solely by dictatorial or authoritarian regimes but in fact China's approach to non-interference has struck a chord even with those democratically elected leaders in Africa. While such practices clearly benefit African elites, it is remains doubtful that they do so for ordinary Africans, although sustained analysis suggests that the potential exists, albeit hampered by the modalities of governance on the continent.

The growing presence of Chinese economic and political actors in Africa reflects what is, perhaps, the most important set of dynamics to shape Africa's external relations since the end of the Cold War. The political dimension of this upsurge in interest from Beijing can be traced from the Tiananmen Square incident in 1989, where China found itself under pressure from its erstwhile economic partners in the West (Taylor 1998, 447). Notably, several African countries rallied around Beijing and expressed support for the measures employed by the Chinese military. In the context where Western powers (temporarily) ostracised Beijing, the Chinese leadership's view of Africa in China's broader foreign policy was subsequently transformed from 'one of benign neglect to one of renewed emphasis ... the developing world was elevated in Chinese thinking to become a "cornerstone" of Beijing's foreign policy' (Taylor 1998, 447).

Beijing found in Africa a supportive constituency. Many African leaders viewed – and continue to view – China as a success story in that it has risen from backwardness to staggering economic growth without following the prescriptions of the West (Alden 2005, 156). Notably, China's leaders have avoided the calls for democracy and good governance that the West ostensibly demands. Equally, China's leadership has in recent years actively courted African leaders with a return to the rhetoric of a shared colonial history of repression. Though this rhetoric harks back to the 1960s and it is doubtful whether it matters that a capitalist exploiter is French, Polish or Chinese (he is still an exploiter), this discourse is lapped up by many African elites, attracted by its intrinsically anti-Western sentiment. A heightened emphasis on the importance of state sovereignty has also chimed with African leaders who have felt under pressure from Western demands for reform. At the same time, the Chinese have seen in Africa a useful arena where it can continue to isolate Taiwan (a struggle China has won hands-down) and as an increasingly important economic resource.

Indeed, the urgent need for oil has been a major impetus in the recent economic surge in Chinese activity in Africa (Shinn and Eisenman 2005, 7). While Beijing has been criticised in Africa that its trade practices significantly benefit the Chinese economy even if this is to the detriment of African countries, the importation of oil from Africa to China has in fact leveled the playing field to a degree between China and Africa. The annual growth rate on the Africa continent has increased in recent years and this is due in large part to the impact of China's economic ventures in the region and its purchase of oil specifically (Taylor 2006, 951). China's renewed interest in Africa has seen many Chinese businesspeople travelling to Africa to pursue their entrepreneurial agendas, and some analysts – as well as many African governments – believe that this will greatly increase the development prospects of local African economies, while also allowing access to a new range of products and services (Tull 2006, 472). Economic growth in Africa has also been furthered by a steady increase in Chinese tourism and this increase has occurred largely through the Chinese government's promotion of many African states as 'officially approved travel destinations,' bringing a much needed boost to the tourism industry in over a dozen countries on the African continent (Alden 2005, 154). Ultimately, it might be said that 'in the short term, China's trade with and investment in Africa are of assistance to the development of the continent, if for no other reason than that little investment is forthcoming from other sources. [Furthermore,] China's investment in Africa's crumbling infrastructure is needed' (Taylor 2006, 949).

In seeking to cultivate external relations with African countries, China has long stressed its commonly shared roots with African nations as a developing country rather than a Western state, and as such 'the symbolic attraction of China, a once-impoverished country victimised by Western imperialism and held back by its own pursuit of disastrous forms of socialism, clearly resonates with African elites looking for a positive development model from the Third World' (Alden 2005, 156). China has provided an economic development model that many African leaders have found to be an attractive alternative to the 'free' and 'open' market economies of both the United States and the European Union (EU). Unlike the aid given to Africa from Western-oriented organisations and countries, Chinese aid rarely comes to Africa with conditional stipulations stressing the importance of tenets such as good governance or a heightened respect for human rights (Tull 2006, 463). Many African elites then have favoured and appreciated such a practice, as this has greatly aided them in legitimising and consolidating their rule (Muekalia 2004, 11). However, it should be noted that this has not been embraced solely by dictatorial or authoritarian regimes but in fact 'China's traditionalist approach to non-interference in domestic affairs accords well with the outlook even of democratically elected leaders in Africa, who view the unity of the state as a sine qua non of effective governance' (Alden 2005, 156). While such practices clearly benefit African elites, it is remains doubtful that they do so for ordinary Africans (Tull 2006, 459).

Contested discourses

In the academic, as well as the political arena, there have been mixed reactions to China's flourishing relations with Africa. One discourse, reflecting the official Chinese view, argues that this partnership will prove to be beneficial for the long-exploited African people in that China is offering a strategic relationship based on mutual benefit, one in which Africa cannot lose. Academics who subscribe to this argument generally talk up how favourable Africans seemingly view China. However, the opposite discourse argues that China, as an ever-aspiring world power, is no different from any other external actor that has shown an interest in cultivating relationships with Africa. By this it is meant that China gains a significant amount more from the relationship than Africa does. In fairness, as Wilson (2005, 7) points out, China and Africa have complementary economic and commercial needs. Africa is short on capital, has a low manufacturing base, is highly import dependent, lacks basic infrastructures and exports a lot of natural resources. China has ample investment capital, a huge manufacturing exporting base, is willing to build infrastructure and imports a significant amount of petroleum and other natural resources. Here, we must be careful to heed Wilson's warning to not generalise Beijing's relationship with a handful of African states to reflect China's ties with the entire African continent.

Having said this, what should Africa be gaining from this increased engagement? If the Chinese promise that it is committed to expanding 'Sino-African trade and economic relations on the basis of *mutual* benefit and win-win cooperation' (Luo Guijin 2006) is to be trusted, then Africa should expect to experience a fundamental surge in economic growth and development, but this remains highly contested and various facets of Sino-African relations reflect both the positive *and* negative aspects of this relationship.

For examples, with regard to trade, Chinese companies and corporations have increasingly begun to look abroad for new markets and Africa has emerged as an attractive destination. Beijing has been keen to promote the idea that China should be given privileged access to African markets on the basis of South-South 'solidarity' and as a concrete manifestation of a broader counter-hegemonic strategy that China is keen to encourage within Africa. The self-serving nature of this stance is obvious. This, coupled with the end of the Multi-Fibre Agreement which had long imposed quotas on Beijing, has meant that cheap Chinese goods, textiles in particular, are flooding Africa markets, causing the academic and political world alike to talk of a textile 'tsunami' (Wilson 2005, 9). This has had a devastating effect on local industry in some countries in various ways. Firstly, most African producers cannot compete with Chinese companies even in Africa's domestic markets, as they are unable to undercut Chinese production costs and prices. Secondly, the growth of Chinese exports to the United States has arguably shut down the promising (albeit artificial) growth of African exports to Washington (Taylor 2009). At present, 'nothing indicates that Africa will be able to compete successfully with China, a result of which is that its exports to China are by and large limited to capital-intensive commodities' (Tull 2006, 472). Tull acknowledges that whilst this is the result of legitimate market competition, it contravenes Beijing's statements that enhanced Chinese–African interaction will always result in win-win situations (*ibid.*). As a consequence, there has been visible domestic reaction by the labour and business sector across the continent, which Kopinski and Polus discuss with regard to the situation in Zambia.

Resource security is undoubtedly the biggest driving force behind China's increased involvement in Africa. Realists would argue that, as an aspiring world power, China is vying to attain material preponderance in order to increase its power and further its campaign for super power status. The volatility of the Middle East, as well as competition from other economies, has forced Beijing to encourage Chinese oil companies to seek other sources of oil to fuel China's rapidly growing economy. Thus Chinese oil companies have turned towards oil producing regions where risks and challenges have meant that the major international companies have overlooked their potential. Africa is one such arguable region. This engagement has had some positive economic impact on the African oil-producing states as the subsequent growth in demand has meant that mineral prices are reaching record highs, reversing a long decline for many of Africa's major exports over the past few decades. For African oil producers, in particular, there has been a substantial windfall. Indeed, as Corkin shows in this volume, African states such as Angola have been quite adept in managing this scenario.

However, the positive implications have the potential to be overshadowed by the negative. Dependency theorists would see Africa as being involved in a classic core-periphery dependency relationship, where the core subordinates and exploits the periphery, whose function it is to supply the former with primary products. The periphery is therefore trapped in a dependent relationship; its economy is entirely reliant on the demand of the core's economy, making it very vulnerable to fluctuations (Taylor 2006, 251). By focusing primarily on exporting natural resources, in particular oil, African states may find themselves open to market shocks which may devastate fragile developing economies. Naidu and Davies (2006, 81) argue that in order to avoid this, Africa must shift its current activities in the natural resource sector towards secondary and tertiary production. Whether this will occur very much depends on the political economies and modalities of governance in various African countries and has little *per se* to do with China.

Motives and messages

China, like any other state, is concerned with advancing itself on the international stage. This means securing energy resources and new markets, in order to drive the Chinese economy. Ultimately, any economic engagements that Beijing undertakes will be with profit securely in mind. However, it is the political context of these economic arrangements that need to be analysed.

At the rhetorical source of the political implications of the Sino-African relationship lie China's Five Principles of Peaceful Coexistence. These effectively lay out how Beijing will conduct its foreign policy, and are: respect for each state's sovereignty; a pact of mutual non-aggression; non-interference in the internal affairs of other states; equality and mutual benefit; and finally, peaceful coexistence with states by seeking common interests. Out of these, it is the policies of non-interference and in turn the respect for sovereignty, which has proven to be the most controversial in the international arena. In a continent that has been wrecked by corrupt and dictatorial leaders, this is a widely criticised political stance. Indeed, critics have suggested that the long-term consequences of Chinese alleged indifference towards the internal affairs of its partners could have problematic results, not least for Chinese business concerns. Yet equally, as Wu Zhengyu and Taylor point out, the policy of strict non-interference is increasingly flexible and is demonstrated through China's increased willingness to partake in peacekeeping operations.

On the international level, it is clear that China is attempting to increase its bargaining power by positioning itself 'at the helm of a coalition of African developing countries' (Muekalia 2004, 10). In doing so, Beijing is hoping to leverage its position on the UN Security Council as well as improving its bargaining power in other international institutions. Beijing is genuinely worried about Washington's long term objectives, and it views any criticism of its domestic policies as imperialist in nature. This concern manifests itself in a search, a 'breaking with the traditional aloofness of Chinese foreign policy' (Alden 2005, 152), for strategic partners. It is in Africa that China has targeted one area where this is to be done. Thus, as China's power and influence grows, Beijing is becoming more and more willing to challenge incumbent powers *and* protect its interests in Africa. As mentioned, the Chinese effectively win over African elites by emphasising South-South solidarity, asserting that China and Africa share identical or similar opinions on many major international affairs as well as common interests. In doing so, China promises to raise the status of African voices on the international level, and this may be partially true. On the political level, Chinese and American competition over Africa *has* enhanced Africa's profile in the international arena. Certainly, in the last few years, Western politicians have placed Africa higher and higher on their agenda. This competition may also allow the African governments to play one power off against the other and thus Africa has regained some of the strategic importance that it had lost after the Cold War.

Whether African governments will take advantage of this position, or squander it, is in the hands of Africans themselves and here the picture is frustrating. China's renewed interest in Africa and the concomitant attention it has provoked from other countries *could* offer African governments the perfect opportunity to exploit the various sides. Ideally, leaders could get their voices heard in the international arena, they could increase the value of foreign aid by getting the donors to actually listen to what is needed and they could utilise the upsurge in receipts to promote development. The fundamental problem, however, lies in the leaders themselves. So long as Africa remains in the grip of corrupt and predatory dictators, these opportunities will always be largely wasted. It is then in the political economy of Africa that one must really look to see how and where China's upsurge in Africa will play out and who will benefit from this engagement and, conversely, who will not.

Overview of the collection

The collection of studies on China–Africa relations starts with Wu Zhengyu and Ian Taylor's contribution on Chinese involvement in peacekeeping in Africa. As the two authors note, China has, in the past decade or so, emerged as an important contributor to UN peacekeeping operations, with Chinese peacekeepers serving in places as diverse as the Democratic Republic of Congo (DRC), Liberia and Sudan. Indeed, China currently sends more peacekeeping troops abroad than any other permanent member of the UN Security Council. This is a major development in Sino-African relations given that historically, Beijing has held a highly hostile attitude towards the notion of 'interference' of any type in a country's affairs. And due to the role of the UN in the Korean War (1950–1953), China's attitude towards the UN sanctioning military missions was, for decades, considerably antagonistic. China's stance on peace operations is – and always has been – closely tied to its attitude on state sovereignty. This has meant that China has set limits on the type of interventions that Beijing is prepared to sanction vis-à-vis its role in peacekeeping missions. Yet it appears that Chinese policy in this regard is evolving. Wu and Taylor discuss why and how China's role in peacekeeping in Africa has played out and the likely directions this is to take in the future.

The discussion then shifts towards the commonly-held idea that China is some sort of voracious 'dragon' intent on grabbing as much of Africa's natural resources as possible and being a pivotal actor in the so-called new scramble for Africa. The security dimensions of this and the suggested possibilities that this will provoke conflict in the future are addressed by Péter Marton and Tamás Matura's study, which notes that Western reactions to China's increasing investment in a number of countries in Africa, as well as Chinese counter-reactions, are often conceptualised as symptoms of a 'honey pot' conflict. Such an impression, as noted, stems from viewing contemporary African development as a 'new scramble' for the continent's natural resources. However, Marton and Matura critically unpack these claims in various fundamental ways, demonstrating how it is untenable. Their objections are based on a survey of Chinese discourses regarding Western criticisms as well empirical objections based on the supposedly 'conflictual' cases of Angola and Sudan, where one in fact finds mutual toleration between Western and Chinese actors. These realities contradict the assumptions of a honey pot conflict. Marton and Matura conclude their analysis with the alternative proposition that any Sino-Western conflict can be more aptly described as partly self-interest-driven, but at the same time normative, and is much more related to Western concerns about a 'spoiler' role played by China in Africa than by any real security threat per se.

The collection then continues with two contributions related to energy issues involving Chinese actors in Africa, with concentrations on two specific case studies: Angola and Zambia. First, Lucy Corkin discusses China's evolving relations with Angola. As she notes, conventional accounts suggest that there exists something entitled the so-called 'Angola Model', whereby the Chinese government is heavily involved in the national reconstruction programme through various financial institutions as a means to ensure closer relations with Angola and thus access to oil. In this light, China's strategy is thus ostensibly to accumulate political capital through the provision of infrastructure, financed by oil-backed concessional loans extended by Chinese state-owned banks. Corkin's study, however, traces the history of China's relations with Angola before examining the various parallel structures involved in the two countries' co-operation over infrastructure, loans and oil. It examines the so-called 'Angola Model' by looking at three key assumptions surrounding risk, access to oil and China's political access in Angola. The study also evaluates the nature of the so-called 'strategic partnership' for both Angola and China. Political posturing indicates that both China and Angola see each other as necessary strategic allies for the foreseeable future, but this may mask an uneasy marriage of convenience. Corkin thus questions the very idea of the 'Angola Model'.

Similarly, Dominik Kopiński and Andrzej Polus question some of the received wisdom about Sino-Zambian relations. They note that Sino-Zambian relations are exceptional to a remarkable degree, and do not seem to fall into the common pattern used to describe the Sino-African relationship as part of a so-called 'new scramble for Africa'. Zambia is a country where both positive and negative developments took place earlier than elsewhere on the African continent and in this respect Zambia has always been one step ahead of the rest of its peers. Kopiński and Polus divide their study into three parts. The first part presents a historical overview of diplomatic relations between China and Zambia. The second part deals with the domestic politics of Zambia and the usage by Zambian elites of the Chinese presence as an argument in internal political discourses. The third part focuses on emerging patterns of Chinese investment in Zambia, and tries to unpack some of the common myths pertaining to the scope and nature of China's engagement in Africa.

The focus of the collection then shifts to looking at how external players fit into the wider Sino-African relationship. Firstly, Karolina Wysoczańska examines Sino-Indian co-operation in Africa, specifically looking at joint efforts between Chinese and Indian actors in Africa's oil sector. As Wysoczańska notes, sourcing sufficient supplies of energy to meet rapidly growing domestic demand is a major challenge for both China and India. The choices these two giants have made to meet that challenge in recent years will have long-term repercussions for the rest of the world. Although efforts to join forces in a global search for energy security are unlikely to overcome deeply ingrained Indian suspicions of China, both countries have already signed a series of energy co-operation agreements, which have indicated that the two states are seeking each other as strategic partners. Wysoczańska provides an overview of the incentives for Sino-Indian co-operation in satisfying domestic oil demands and also examines the implications of such collaboration on regional and global orders.

Maurizio Carbone then follows with his study of how the EU and China variously compete in Africa. Carbone analyses the impact of China's rise in Africa on the EU. Contrary to conventional wisdom, he argues that the EU's renewed interest in Africa is not the result of China's new assertiveness in the continent, but is a consequence of the intensive search for a more coherent external policy by Brussels, something which has been in place since the early 2000s. According to Carbone, Africa represents an ideal venue in which different EU actors could simultaneously pursue traditional development goals together with new political objectives. However, the existence of three competing visions within the EU have negatively affected its ability to constructively engage with China: the European Commission has sought to affirm the EU's aspiration to become an influential global actor; the European Parliament has projected its preference for a value-based development policy, blended with paternalistic overtones; and the Council of the EU has been driven more by the emotional reactions of some member states, who have not wanted to lose their position as Africa's main reference point. Unsurprisingly, the result has been a confused message which China has found hard to follow, never mind Africa, since they were not effectively involved in the process and were sceptical about the whole idea of 'trilateral cooperation'.

Finally, Łukasz Fijałkowski critiques the notion of China's 'soft power' in Africa. He notes that Beijing's political 'charm offensive' in Africa has ostensibly made China a major player on the continent. The source of this success in China's African policy is sometimes attributed to China's political and economic 'attractiveness'. Whilst it is true that China is building a positive image targeted to the audience in Africa, promoting for example the vision of 'win-win' mutual economic benefits from cooperation and so this in part might be viewed as being close to the concept of soft power, soft power is much more about about dynamic relationships between agent and the subject of attraction. Hence, as Fijałkowski asserts, the general growth of Chinese soft power and its success depends not only on whether China can sell its image to African states, but also whether African states are willing to buy this.

As might be noted, a large part of the contributions are from scholars based in, or from, Central Europe. After a hiatus in the post-Cold War era, when African Studies were downgraded by all of the ex-Warsaw Pact nations, African Studies is becoming more popular and is increasingly attracting younger scholars from Central Europe, who conduct fieldwork and detailed academic work. The proposed and imminent establishment of an African Studies Centre at the University of Wrocław in Poland, a centre to serve the central European region, demonstrates the emerging importance of Africa back on the academic agenda in the former Eastern Bloc countries. This development is something that all Africanists, wherever they are based, should welcome. This collection of essays is thus, in part, an effort to showcase this renaissance of interest in Africa and demonstrate the type of scholarly work on Africa being conducted by academics from that part of Europe.

References

Alden, C. 2005. China in Africa. *Survival* 47, no. 3: 147–64.
Guijin, L. 2006. Address by the Chinese Ambassador to South Africa, Liu Guijin at the African Business Leaders Forum: 'Economic and Trade Relations between China and Africa Anchored on Mutual Benefit', Pretoria: Embassy of the People's Republic of China.
Muekalia, D. 2004. Africa and China's strategic partnership. *African Security Review* 13, no. 1: 5–11.
Naidu, S., and M. Davies. 2006. China fuels its future with Africa's riches. *South African Journal of International Affairs* 13, no. 2: 69–83.
Shinn, D., and J. Eisenman. 2005. Dueling priorities for Beijing in the horn of Africa. *China Brief* 5, no. 21: 1–4.
Taylor, I. 1998. China's foreign policy towards Africa in the 1990s. *Journal of Modern African Studies* 36, no. 3: 443–60.
Taylor, I. 2006. China's oil diplomacy in Africa. *International Affairs* 82, no. 5: 937–59.
Taylor, I. 2009. *China's new role in Africa*. Boulder: Lynne Rienner.
Tull, D. 2006. China's engagement in Africa: Scope, significance and consequences. *Journal of Modern African Studies* 44, no. 3: 459–79.
Wilson, E. 2005. China's influence in Africa: Implications for U.S. Policy. Testimony Before the Sub-Committee on Africa, Human Rights and International Operations. Washington DC: House of Representatives, 28 July.

From refusal to engagement: Chinese contributions to peacekeeping in Africa

Wu Zhengyu[a] and Ian Taylor[a,b,1]

[a]*Renmin University of China, China;* [b]*University of St Andrews, Scotland, UK/University of Stellenbosch, South Africa*

> China has, in the past decade or so, emerged as an important contributor to United Nations (UN) peacekeeping operations, with Chinese peacekeepers serving in places as diverse as the Democratic Republic of Congo (DRC), Liberia and Sudan. Indeed, China currently sends more peacekeeping troops abroad than any other permanent member of the UN Security Council. This is a major development in Sino-African relations. China's stance on peace operations is closely tied to its attitude on state sovereignty and this limits the type of interventions that Beijing is prepared to sanction vis-à-vis its role in peacekeeping missions. Yet it appears that Chinese policy in this regard is evolving. This study discusses why and how China's role in peacekeeping in Africa has played out and the likely directions this is to take in the future.

Since 1990, China has contributed over 7,000 peacekeepers to United Nations (UN) operations, and Chinese peacekeepers have served in places such as the Democratic Republic of Congo (DRC), Liberia and Sudan. In fact, China currently sends more peacekeeping troops abroad than any other permanent member of the UN Security Council. Wang Guangya, China's UN ambassador, has noted that 'China is filling a vacuum left by the West. The major powers are withdrawing from the peacekeeping role. That role is being played more by small countries. China felt it is the right time for us to fill this vacuum' (*Washington Post,* 24 November 2006).

The number of Chinese military personnel sent on peace missions has been growing in recent years and is a major development in Sino-African relations. However, China's stance on peace operations is closely tied to its attitude on state sovereignty and this limits the type of interventions that Beijing is prepared to sanction vis-à-vis its role in peacekeeping missions. The most remarkable feature of China's 'flurry of UN peacekeeping' efforts in the post-Cold War era has been its focus on the 'domestic political scene' of the countries where the Chinese contribute to peace operations (James 1993, 359). This study discusses why and how this has played out as China has become more and more involved in peacekeeping operations in Africa.

State sovereignty

It has long been a central tenet of Chinese foreign policy post-1949 that the normative principles of state sovereignty and non-interference must serve as the bases for international relations between states. Though this position is shifting somewhat, as Beijing's growing involvement in peace operations demonstrate, this remains fundamental. China's valorisation of sovereignty springs from its experiences in the nineteenth and early twentieth centuries. This Century of Humiliation, in popular Chinese parlance, lasted from the First Opium War in 1839 to the triumph of the Communist Party of China (CPC) in 1949 when, per Mao Zedong, the Chinese people stood up *(zhongguo renmin zhancilai le)*. China guards its sovereignty as a correlative of 'regaining' its 'rightful place' in international affairs (Elegant 1963): 'The attainment of ... great-power aspirations ... draws upon strong emotions, linked to nationalist sentiments, traditional cultural ethnocentrism, and a deeply rooted sense of injustice at the hands of ... (especially) Western countries' (Swaine 1995, 84).

In addition, China has traditionally emphasised the right of states to resolve issues among themselves, in keeping with its resistance to outside involvement in affairs it perceives as strictly domestic, such as those of Tibet and Taiwan.[2] As Pang Zhongying (2005, 88) notes, 'Central to Chinese concerns is the changing nature and context of peace operations – with the potential for mission creep and the move to 'coalitions of the willing' – and the implications [these] would have for international involvement in China's key internal affairs relating, for example, to Taiwan, Tibet, and Xinjiang'. Beijing has scrupulously avoided establishing international precedents that could later be used to justify interference in China's so-called domestic issues.

However, we should emphasise that the rhetoric contained in official Chinese pronouncements 'has led many observers to reach the premature conclusion that Beijing opposes all forms of intervention and is wedded to an antiquated approach to sovereignty' (Carlson 2006, 218). In fact, it is possible to discern a subtle shift in China's position regarding state sovereignty.[3] Consider, for instance, the evolution of four its official guidelines on legitimate intervention. These state that intervening bodies must first proceed with respect for the concerned state's sovereignty. Second, they must gain the authorisation of the UN. Third, they must secure an invitation from the concerned state. Finally, they should use force only when all other options have proven ineffective (Carlson 2004). This set of necessary conditions demonstrates that Beijing has softened its hard-line stance on state sovereignty and non-interference.

Yet the Westphalian notion that interference requires an invitation holds even in the event that the host government has embarked on widespread and systematic killing or territorial cleansing. By implication, such governments can veto intervention. In the past, when foreign troops intervened in the affairs of a state at the behest of its government, China based its opinion of the legality of the action on whether the official request corresponded to the genuine desires of 'the people' as it saw them. This qualification, of course, permitted China to decide legality on the basis of political expediency. China has now effectively abandoned this position and currently focuses on a legalistic interpretation of state sovereignty in the face of intervention. The will of the people is not part and parcel of China's diplomacy or decision-making process in this regard.

Perhaps to avoid such potential conundrums, China has become quite adept at pursuing a strategy of nonparticipation or abstention from Security Council debates and votes on peace operations. It can in fact be argued that abstention is an expedient strategy for China, since it precludes both criticism from the West regarding obstructionist opposition to contentious peace operations *and* criticism from the developing world, allowing China either to disassociate itself from controversial operations or to remain in accordance with its doctrine of non-interference even with respect to popular peace operations.

The changing nature of United Nations' peacekeeping operations (UNKPOs) has itself made abstention an important tool of Chinese diplomacy. Under Chapter VII, the Security Council is allowed to take coercive action, including military force, against a state (Article 42) if the Council concludes that it has made 'any threat to the peace, breach of the peace, or act of aggression' (Article 39). The notion of state sovereignty 'shall not prejudice the application of enforcement measures under Chapter VII' (per Chapter I, Article 2). This article is a problem for Beijing, which has had to face several similarly thorny issues in the era following the Brahimi Report, issued in 2000 by a high-level panel chaired by former Algerian foreign minister Lakhdar Brahimi and reviewed all facets of UN peacekeeping operations. The report made four significant proposals:

1. Peacekeepers need to be expressly mandated to be able to use force more advantageously to defend themselves, their mission *and* civilians under threat of attack.
2. The UN should never mandate a peace operation prior to marshalling the necessary resources to execute the mission.
3. There needs to be improved discussion between the Security Council and the contributing countries to any peace operation.
4. A diversified approach to peacebuilding, including the training of local police, strengthening the legal machinery in post-conflict states, disarmament, demobilisation, and reintegration of former soldiers and the advancement of human rights – basically the construction of liberal-democratic states under the rubric of what might be termed the liberal peace. (United Nations Secretary-General 2000)

Post-Brahimi, peace support emerged as a novel type of peacekeeping. The Brahimi Report effectively codified changes that had been occurring since the end of the Cold War. While providing a new framework and approach, it fundamentally reflected events and debates that had been going on since at least 1990. Importantly, it was understood that this framework amounted to clear authorisation for the deployment of military force to pressurise warring sides to abide by established peace agreements, although UN peace operations (also known as blue-helmet operations) still only deploy with host government consent. While the Brahimi Report did not legitimise intervention and indeed confined itself to talking about peace operations, it nonetheless dictated that blue-helmet troops deployed in peace operations could not stand by in the face of civilian massacres. But even this concession raised ire among the Chinese, as the argument of one scholar illustrates:

Will the out-of-control 'humanitarian intervention' become a reprint [sic] of the globalisation of colonialism in the twenty-first century? ... [The colonialists] didn't take into account [the] rights and ideas of people of the colonies in Asia, Africa, and Latin America at all. And today, it is these former colonial countries that [have] their hedge of sovereignty [sic] being breached in the process of the generalising of 'humanitarian intervention' (Qin Xiaocheng 2003, 169).

Ultimately, however, the Brahimi Report represented (and reflected) a shift from traditional peacekeeping actions to peace-support missions as the UN took a more active role in upholding international peace and security as well as in member-states' affairs. For the Chinese, traditional peacekeeping 'is organised and deployed directly by the UN with the consent of all parties' (Zhang Li 2003, 209). 'All parties' in this context refers to state actors. In contrast, the Brahimi Report urged consent from the host government but not necessarily from all the parties involved, a provision Beijing felt comfortable with, as the 2002 Chinese Defence White Paper illustrates: 'China supports the active measures taken by the UN Secretariat in this regard and welcomes the progress made by the UN General Assembly and the Security Council in deliberating the Brahimi Report on Reforming the UN's Peacekeeping Operations' (Information Office of the State Council 2002). This move has had implications for the evolution of China's peacekeeping commitments in Africa and elsewhere.

The evolution of China's involvement in peace operations

According to He Yin (2007), there have been four phases in the evolution of Beijing's attitude toward peace operations. The first phase, lasting from 1971 to 1980, was characterised by inactivity if not outright hostility with respect to such missions. The second phase reflected a gradual change in attitude from 1981 to 1987. The third period, from 1988 to 1989, saw Chinese cooperate in some UN peace operations while issuing a fair number of challenges toward others. And the fourth period, from 1999 onwards, is marked by greater and greater Chinese participation in operations, despite some remaining reservations on certain issues.

In the first phase, China avoided playing any role in UN peacekeeping missions and did not even contribute to their costs. We should remember, however, that China was the object of the first US-led enforcement mission sanctioned by the Security Council in 1951. Thereafter Beijing saw all UN interventions as superpower chicanery aimed at weaker states within the international system. This suspicion – compounded by the memory of the Korean War – lasted well past the era of Mao. Indeed, in 1990, then Foreign Minister Qian Qichen stated that Beijing's reluctance to support the enforcement mission in Iraq sprang from the fact that 'the Chinese people still clearly remember that the Korean War was launched in the name of the United Nations' (quoted in Kim 1995, 423). Consequently 'most of such UN actions were seen as interference in countries' internal affairs and as the undesirable result of US-Soviet hegemonic power competition' (Wang Jianwei 1999, 70). What is more, the People's Republic of China (PRC) was emerging from the Cultural Revolution at the time, so issues of Chinese diplomatic capacity within the UN system cannot be underestimated.

Conversely, upon joining the UN, China was often accused of free riding off of the international community and avoiding its global responsibilities as a permanent member of the Security Council. Indeed, China was charged with being a group of one, uninterested in contributing to world order but reaping all the benefits of thereof (Kim 1995). It was not until the 1980s that Beijing's overall attitude toward the UN began to evolve. Interestingly, however, when China did begin to play a more active role, some in the West feared that it would represent the more conservative, old-fashioned opposition to those in favour of the evolving form of peacekeeping that was more forceful and involved potential interference in the domestic affairs of recipient nations.

While the traditional peacekeeping initially favoured by China may still have its place after Brahimi – for example, in conflicts like the Ethiopian-Eritrean border war – it would not really work in contemporary civil wars, as exemplified by Darfur. Given that Chinese foreign policy has long been predicated on the Five Principles of Peaceful Coexistence, which includes a strong normative commitment to non-interference, Beijing's increasing willingness to play an active role in peacekeeping missions is indeed intriguing. It has certainly begun to shape an aspect of China's Africa policy hitherto ignored by most commentators.

Initially, upon entering the UN in 1971, China maintained its vehement opposition to all peacekeeping operations, refusing to take part in Security Council votes on resolutions pertaining to peace operations and going so far as to refuse to pay the yearly peacekeeping contributions expected of it as a member of the Security Council. Contributing troops to peace operations was certainly out of the question: 'Based upon Mao's theory of just war, China viewed peacekeeping as an act of superpower 'power politics,' a pretext deployed to justify US or Soviet intervention in the affairs of small states' (Fravel 1996, 1104).

To trace the evolution in Chinese thinking more specifically, in 1981, as China's modernisation project was continuing apace, China voted in favour of such peace-keeping resolutions as an extension of the UN mission in Cyprus and also began to disburse its annual peacekeeping contribution. It thereafter supported every resolution on UN peace operations from 1981 to 1990 (Morphet 2000). This policy change sprang from the adoption of an 'independent foreign policy of peace' *(duli zizhu de heping waijiao zhengce)* which the CPC inscribed into the PRC's revised constitution at the Twelfth National Congress in 1982 and reflected policymakers' awareness that China needed a stable and peaceful world in which to realise its plans for economic development and modernisation. '"Peace" mean[t] that China began to formulate its foreign policy from the viewpoint of whether it [was] beneficial to international and regional peace instead of [to the pursuit of] military superiority, while "independence" mean[t] that China began to formulate its foreign policy according to its national interests and the common interests of peoples of all the countries in the world' (Xia Liping 2001, 18). This included maintaining 'equidistant' relations with the United States and the Soviet Union as well as a 'more positive [attitude toward] UN affairs' in general (Pang Zhongying 2005, 90).

Equally, the policy allowed China to pose as a counterbalance to the superpowers in the name of the developing world, where peace operations were most likely to take place. However, Beijing was still 'stak[ing] out a particularly narrow interpretation of the international community's right to intervene ... predicated upon an interpretation of sovereignty as a virtually scared right of states' (Carlson 2006, 221).

Yet as the 1990s developed, Beijing reluctantly began to accept the development of trends in international politics that militated against this hard-line stance. According to a *China Daily* article by Wu Miaofa of the China Institute of International Studies

(29 May 2007), China changed its tack for three key reasons. First, Beijing became conscious of the fact that UN peacekeeping operations were 'an important means of maintaining international peace and security', for although 'many of the long-standing conflicts [could not] be permanently resolved by peacekeeping efforts alone ... peacekeeping [could] alleviate crises and provide strong support for developing countries suffering from a lack of allies as well as their own weaknesses'. Second, Wu noted that a Chinese analysis of peacekeeping operations 'carried out from 1948 to 2000 showed that a total of 54 missions concerning 52 countries mostly involved developing nations'. Since 'some developing countries also joined peacekeeping operations, including seven African, six Asian, and six Latin American nations', and since 'quite a few commanders of peacekeeping troops were from developing countries', China was, in Wu's view, motivated to change its policy by its self-image as the de facto leader of the developing world. Finally:

> As one of the permanent members of the UN Security Council, China reassessed its position in the international system and concluded: despite undesirable aspects, the current international order [could] drive the growth of productivity; it remain[ed] a long-term task to build a new international political and economic order; [and thus] China should join other developing countries in pushing the international political and economic order in a more sensible direction. This included using the UN peacekeeping mechanism (*ibid.*).

As China's economic and political clout continue to grow, Chinese policymakers are also gaining confidence, which enables them to commit to selective involvement in international affairs. Peacekeeping is no exception.

The Chinese are also interested in gaining experience by participating in the UN and its peace operations (He Yin 2007). In fact, Drew Thompson (2005) identifies several important benefits China derives from taking part in UN peace operations. First, participation enhances Beijing's authority not only in regions where Chinese peacekeepers operate but also on the UNSC and among other voting members of the UN as well, not least those representing Africa – who are thus all the more likely to continue providing useful support in times of difficulty.

Second, China's reputation as a responsible world power is enhanced by involvement in peace operations; as 'the most self-conscious rising power in history ... and is desperate to be seen as a benign force' (*Christian Science Monitor*, 27 June 2007). Third, by participating in peace operations, China increases its strategic presence in regions, particularly within Africa, whose resources may prove crucial for meeting China's energy needs.

Furthermore, as noted earlier, China is also filling a prominent vacuum left by Western members of the UNSC who contribute financially to peace operations but generally shy away from committing significant troop numbers. As Bonny Ling (2007, 48) notes, 'This has undoubtedly enhanced China's strategic positioning at the UN, especially since peacekeeping is the single most high-profile element of any UN activities on the ground'.

China took part in its first UNPKO in 1988, having joined the UN Special Committee on Peacekeeping Operations (UNSCPO) shortly after UN peacekeeping forces had received the Nobel Prize for Peace (Staehle 2006). The following year it sent non-military personnel to observe Namibia's general elections and, in 1990, it sent five military observers to join the United Nations Truce Supervision

Organisation (UNTSO) in the Middle East. Later, in 1993, Beijing approved the UN Transitional Authority in Cambodia (UNTAC), not only financing a good part of the operation but also sending in a military unit. These moves represented a 'significant departure from [China's] past behaviour in multilateral diplomacy for collective security purposes' (Wang Jianwei 1999, 76). In fact, 'since the early 1990s, the Chinese ... [have] consistently finessed the meaning of these principles [regarding sovereignty] in order to create a rhetorical space for [their] acquiescence in various "Western"-sponsored UN operations' (Carlson 2006, 218) as a way to break out of the temporary diplomatic isolation encountered after Tiananmen Square in 1989 (Roy 1998, 147–48).

Nevertheless, China remained cautious in its attitude toward peacekeeping, restating its opposition to the use of force whenever it overrode the sovereignty of a state. Beginning in the mid-1990s, 'Beijing saw problems as the lines between peacekeeping and peacemaking became fuzzier; as expansion was accompanied by civilian missions concerned with human rights, refuges, and inspections; and as these missions had less-than-complete support from host nations' (Gill 2007, 116); in the words of one Western academic, it 'seemed that an era might be dawning in which Western governments, freed from the constraints of the Cold War, would use their armies to save strangers in places far from home' (Wheeler 2000, 172). Consequently, China's 'involvement in UNTAC was not repeated in subsequent missions. This was partly due to [its] attitude toward the principles of state sovereignty and its concern about the use of force in peacekeeping operations. These issues only served to highlight the emerging contradictions and ambiguities with regard to China's position on the nature of peace operations' (Pang Zhongying 2005, 91).

As a result, China opposed features of Operation Provide Comfort in Iraqi Kurdistan, UN Protection Force (UNPROFOR) in Yugoslavia, Operation Turquoise in Rwanda and Operation Restore Democracy in Haiti – all by abstaining on the Security Council resolutions to authorise or expanding them (Carlson 2006, 224). China was clearly taking a rearguard action against contemporary peace operations insofar as they involved military enforcement, while supporting traditional peacekeeping operations. It was, for all intents and purposes, a stance against 'mission creep', which China believed meant that 'the United Nations was becoming an instrument of "hegemonism"' (Gill 2007, 116).

In the run-up to the first Gulf War (1990–1991), Beijing was supportive of Chapter VII's resolutions concerning Iraq, though it expended a great deal of energy working to take out recommendations specifying military force (Staehle 2006). When the UN did approve Resolution 678, entailing the deployment of all necessary means including military force, China abstained. However, as part of its effort to rebuild its international image post-1989, Beijing continued to support traditional peacekeeping missions such as the 1994 UN Operation in Mozambique (ONUMOZ), which it saw as demonstrating the efficacy of traditional peacekeeping; as a Chinese commentary put it: 'The experience of ONUMOZ has proved that as long as the two parties to the conflict are sincere about resolving their problems through negotiations and unswervingly implement the agreements reached by the parties, it is highly possible for them, with the help of the international community, to end yesterday's suffering and open up a new vista' (quoted in Choedon 2005, 43).

However, China had more difficulty determining what to do when said parties resisted the implementation of peace agreements.[4] China has in general opposed deviation from Chapter I (Article 4 that opposes the use of force 'against the territorial integrity or political independence of any state') and Chapter VI of the UN Charter that requires from peacekeeping operations impartiality of the peacekeeping forces, the consent of the parties involved in the dispute, the use of means other than force to keep the peace, and the prior agreement to a ceasefire between the parties concerned. These remain the legal basis for China's support for peacekeeping operations and, naturally, their violation forms the basis for Chinese opposition.[5]

Yet it should be noted that one of China's first peacekeeping roles in Africa involved support of the United Task Force (UNITAF) and its UN Operation in Somalia (UNOSOM). UNOSOM was organised to monitor the ceasefire between warlords, despite the fact that they were still engaging in violence and that humanitarian assistance was under threat from looting and abuse by their militias.

It was the interception of humanitarian aid that led to the authorisation of the UNITAF mission under Chapter VII. China supported UNITAF but made clear that it considered the situation exceptional, as anarchy was raging in the absence of any government in Mogadishu – a key point as far as it was concerned. Beijing's position was influenced by the fact that it 'did not want to be perceived as obstructionist by casting vetoes on Somalia-related UNSC resolutions and hindering humanitarian assistance. This was especially true since it already had a bad image abroad, especially in the West, following the 1989 Tiananmen incident' (He Wenping 2007, 29).

Once UNITAF had completed its mission, Beijing supported UNOSOM II, again under Chapter VII and again on the grounds that Somalia constituted a temporary exception and that normal peacekeeping operations should be resumed as soon as possible. However, once fighting between UN troops and Somali militias began – culminating in the infamous Black Hawk Down incident – China backtracked. For instance, the *Beijing Review* asserted that 'the torturous experience in Somalia has taught the lesson that peacekeeping must be limited to peacekeeping. The internal affairs of one country can be solved only by the people of that country. The efforts of the international community can only be helpful or supplementary' (quoted in Fravel 1996, 1114). Assistant Minister of Foreign Affairs Li Zhaoxing likewise stated that 'the fundamental and effective way to settle the Somali question is by peaceful means. Resort to coercive military actions will only serve to complicate matters' (*ibid.*, 1113–4).

Crucially, the Mogadishu debacle resulted in a de facto refusal by Washington to get involved in efforts to stop the 1994 genocide in Rwanda. While the United States and other Western powers have been (rightly) lambasted for resisting calls to intervene, criticism of China, which was equally resistant to getting involved, has been muted.[6] In fact, it was only in June 1994 that a multinational force was authorised under Chapter VII to stabilise the situation (although the French actually started deploying before the Resolution was passed). The United Nations Assistance Mission for Rwanda (UNAMIR) did not reach the military numbers it required to deploy until much later. China abstained from the vote, even though the resolution authorising the Chapter VII mandate emphasised the temporary and unique nature of the mission, on the grounds that the mission did not have the approval of all parties involved in the fighting – granting the *genocidaires* an implicit veto on the vote to stop their butchering.

In May 1997, China agreed in principle to contribute to the UN Department of Peacekeeping Operations (DPKO). However, that same year, it was active in warning against the intrusion into the domestic affairs of African countries under the guise of peace operations; it backed the establishment of the United Nations Observer Mission in Angola (MONUA) but expressed concern that the military element of the mission might get drawn into issues that should by rights concern other UN departments. Wang Xue Xian, China's UNSC representative, stated at the time that 'as a principle, the Security Council should not get involved in those activities which fall under the terms of reference of other United Nations bodies' and that 'China had reservations on certain elements of the draft resolution and on aspects of the observer mission's mandate' (quoted in United Nations Security Council 1997).

China had similar concerns with the United Nations Mission in the Central African Republic (MINURCA), which aimed to stabilise and restructure the republic's military. In a vote to extend MINURCA's mandate, China's UNSC representative, Lin Chengxun, while supportive, observed that although 'the mission had played a great role and ... demonstrated that the Security Council could do concrete work for African countries and people ... reforms, especially the restructuring of the armed forces, [are] the internal affairs of a country. Therefore, the Council should not intervene too much in that area' (quoted in United Nations Security Council 1999).

The events in Kosovo in 1998 and 1999 particularly worried Beijing as NATO's air campaign served to flag for Chinese policymakers the dangers of non-UN-mandated interferences in domestic affairs. Beijing was absolutely against the NATO campaign, deeming the whole exercise deeply problematic if not ominous. Indeed, after the Chinese embassy in Belgrade was hit by NATO missiles on 7 May 1999, indignant, anti-Western nationalism proved difficult to contain;

> The view from China's capital was that the United States – the main organiser and contributor of the coalition – was bent on enforcing its vision of proper global order on the rest of the world, even if the attainment of this goal required armed aggression (Dreyer 2000, 3).

Yet the Kosovo campaign may have served as a positive catalyst for changes in China's policies, as 'the shock of [it] and especially the embassy bombing compelled Chinese strategists to seek new ways to ensure Chinese influence over the methods and processes of international intervention' (Gill and Reilly 2000, 48). This shift helps explain China's support for a 1999 mandate for the UN Mission in Sierra Leone (UNAMSIL) to implement a Disarmament, Demobilisation, and Reintegration (DDR) programme, support elections and smooth the transfer of aid to the country (Staehle 2006, 41). UNAMSIL was authorised under Chapter VII to ensure the safety of its personnel and to defend civilians but acknowledged the rights and responsibilities of the government of Sierra Leone, which in turn fully supported the mission. Thus China was likewise more than willing to support it. Protecting the distribution of humanitarian aid and patrolling strategic locations within Sierra Leone were clearly compatible with China's stance on peacekeeping.

In subsequent missions, China collaborated on peace-support operations in the DRC, Liberia, Côte d'Ivoire, Burundi and the Sudan (as we will see), since they all explicitly limited military force to the defence of UN personnel and civilians in impending danger and 'interference' in domestic affairs was not an issue. In short,

China agreed to peace-support operations with elements of peace enforcement, provided they were carefully restricted.

However, as the UNSC has adopted an increasingly broad interpretation of what constitutes a threat under Chapter VII, China's position has become increasingly complicated.[7] Beijing still insists on securing the blessing of the host country before authorising operations based on human-rights infringements. Thus China unambiguously supported the UN Organisation Mission in the Democratic Republic of Congo (MONUC), which was created with Kinshasa's approval after the signing of the Lusaka Ceasefire Agreement in 1999. MONUC is authorised under Chapter VII to take the necessary measures to improve security in North and South Kivu and the Ituri district, where the UNSC had identified serious human-rights abuses. Importantly for China, the Congolese government was a key signatory of the original agreement for the cessation of hostilities in the DRC and hence a willing host nation of MONUC – however limited in practical terms its reach may have been in the areas in question. China's position relied on the literal definition of 'host nation' *(dangshi guo)* used in it's the Defence White Paper of 2002 (a revision of the 1998 White Paper), namely 'the state that is a party' (Information Office of the State Council 2002). This definition suggests that that the consent of all parties to UN involvement is not absolutely necessary, a qualification that is important 'where state authority is either highly disputed or effectively nonexistent', as in the case of the DRC (Gill and Reilly 2000, 44).

In stark contrast is the case of Darfur, where Beijing opposed the initial efforts to involve outsiders in improving the security conditions. Thus, whereas the UN Mission in Sudan (UNMIS) had functioned in southern Sudan since early 2005, it took considerable efforts – often in the teeth of Chinese opposition – for a mission to be sent to operate in Darfur. Initially, only a somewhat lacklustre effort by the African Union (AU) was allowed by Khartoum, with Beijing continually backing up the Sudanese refusal to allow a more intrusive and fully international mission. This continued even after it became clear that the AU's ability to defend Darfurians was negligible, as Beijing continued to insist it would back peace-support operations only with an invitation from the host country.[8]

However, since late 2006 Beijing began to exhibit an increased willingness to engage with the international community on Darfur and started to apply pressure on Khartoum to modify its behaviour and engage in a political process for the peaceful resolution of the Darfur conflict. This change in policy by Beijing was mainly due to overwhelming international criticism of China's role in Sudan and the increasing reputational costs that Beijing was experiencing by being closely associated with Khartoum. Subsequently, Beijing voted for UNSC Resolution 1769 that created a hybrid United Nations African Mission in Darfur (UNAMID). While it was the case that China at times went along with the Sudanese government's opposition to its full implementation, by mid-June 2008, Hu Jintao strongly urged Sudan to cooperate in allowing the deployment of peacekeeping forces into Darfur as part of UNAMID, clearly indicating that the limits of Chinese patience had been reached. Indeed, in a meeting with Sudan's vice-president, Ali Uthman Muhammad Taha, Hu was reported to have used unusually frank language in calling on Khartoum to try harder to settle the conflict in Darfur. This was in the context whereby 26,000 peacekeepers were supposed to have been deployed in Darfur, but no more than half that number had arrived on the ground by mid-2008, mainly due to intransigence by Khartoum. According to one report:

> Hu's comments and their prominent publication ... are part of an increasingly open Chinese diplomatic campaign to persuade Sudanese leaders to cooperate more with international efforts to end the fighting in Darfur .... China has come under criticism from human rights activists for failing to pressure Khartoum forcefully enough [and] the official portrayal of [the] meeting was seen as a departure from China's usual style of quiet diplomacy and ritual proclamations of friendship (*Washington Post*, 13 June 2008).

Thus there has been a clear movement in China's position on peacekeeping operations – one which has departed from the hard-and-fast defence of sovereignty and non-interference which is usually characterised as marking out Chinese foreign policy.[9]

Ambivalence and evolution

China has long been circumspect about intervening in other countries' affairs even when sanctioned by the UN and remains suspicious that the UNSC authorises Chapter VII mandates too readily.[10] However, as Beijing has emerged as an economic superpower it has been compelled to embark on a change of direction in some aspects of its foreign policy. One such shift is from an absolute refusal to support peace operations under any circumstances to a permanent commitment to doing so. China is now a major contributor of UN peacekeepers, most of whom are in Africa (three-quarters of all Chinese personnel deployed under the UN serve in Africa). It also maintains two training facilities for peacekeeping personnel: one in Nanjing, Jiangsu province, and the other in Langfang, Hebei. And in August 2007 it was announced that Major-General Zhao Jingmin would be appointed force commander for MINURSO, making him the first Chinese national to head a UN mission (*Xinhua*, 28 August 2007).

In many ways, Beijing has had international leadership pushed upon it. As China's economy has exponentially expanded and its trade profile has increased across the globe, expectations that Beijing would (and should) play a greater role in international relations has been almost axiomatic. Furthermore, in considering questions of domestic security, 'China has gradually realised that peacekeeping missions can help to secure a peaceful international environment, which works in China's national interest as the country begins to build a sound external environment for its long-term economic growth and social development' (Pang Zhongying 2005, 97).

China's increased profile, particularly in Africa, has led to criticism, including charges of neo-colonialism, that Beijing's foreign policy makers are attempting to counteract. Acutely aware of its global reputation, China is taking part in peace operations as one way to project a more benign and even positive image. As Dai Shao'an, vice-director of the Peacekeeping Affairs Office of the Ministry of Defence, has put it, 'wherever they go or whatever they do, [Chinese peacekeepers] always bear in mind that they are messengers of peace, representing China .... To win hearts and minds, you need to devote your own hearts and minds, and that is exactly what our peacekeepers are doing' (*China Daily*, 24 July 2007). A Chinese academic agrees that 'active participation [in peace operations] is a demonstration of China's commitment to the UN and its security functions as mandated by the UN Charter. It is not only useful for serving China's moral cause or fulfilling its international responsibility in the post–Cold War era. It also provides an arena in which China can learn to interact with the international community in ways commensurate with its status as a rising power' (Pang Zhongying 2005, 87). Playing a role in Africa is particularly important for China, explains Elizabeth Economy from the Council on Foreign Relations, as it attempts to reassure the world that it is not motivated solely by its need for resources: 'It has a number of reputational risks. Being seen as a force for peace and security is an important and good first step' (quoted in *Washington Post*, 24 November 2006).

Beijing is now steadily constructing a reputation for being at the forefront of conflict resolution in Africa, even if the numbers it actually contributes to various peace operations is small.[11] In fact, China has been relatively successful in projecting a positive diplomatic image vis-à-vis peace operations in Africa, earning the praise of various African commentators. Liberian president Ellen Johnson-Sirleaf, for instance, commended China for supporting Liberia in its peacekeeping, asserting that 'Liberians will never forget the friendship of Chinese peacekeeping soldiers' (*People's Daily*, 1 February 2007).

Interestingly, it was the Chinese who urged other nations to support the deployment of peacekeepers to Somalia during a UNSC mission to Addis Ababa in June 2006 – 'the first time [China] had taken the lead in the fifteen nation council in promoting foreign intervention to resolve a conflict thousands of miles from its own borders' (*Washington Post*, 24 November 2006). According to Chinese reports, African governments pressed China to raise the issue with the Council. However, Princeton Lyman – a former US ambassador with expertise on Sino-African ties – has a more prosaic view, namely that China is seeking to score diplomatic points by supporting vital regional allies such as Ethiopia, which had itself sent thousands of troops to Somalia to protect the official interim government (*Washington Post*, 24 November 2006).

Conclusion

It appears that an increasingly important aspect of China's African policy involves peacekeeping. Where it will lead remains open to question. The lack of strategic trust between China and many Western countries with regard to military involvement – including peacekeeping – around the world, not least in Africa, is problematic.[12] China is highly sceptical about the motives behind much Western interest in peace operations and understandably rejects US leadership at the UN and/or US interpretation of international relations.[13] China has always couched its concerns in terms of hegemony, and there is little evidence to suggest it will do otherwise in the future. Indeed, following the NATO military strikes against Yugoslavia in the spring of 1999, one Chinese commentator wrote, that 'Hegemonism and power politics are still developing, and there will be no peace under heaven in the twenty-first century' (*Liaowang*, 17 May 1999). Wang Jincun, a senior researcher at the Chinese Academy of Social Sciences similarly asserted in an article titled 'Global democratisation – camouflage of US hegemony' that 'what deserves more attention is that the United States, not yet satisfied with its Cold War achievements, seeks to gain more advances through military means .... The military interference by the United States in Iraq,

Somalia, Haiti, and Bosnia-Herzegovina, the bombing against Sudan and Afghanistan, and especially the ongoing air strikes against Yugoslavia serve as prominent examples' (*Xinhua,* 27 May 1999).

China remains resolute in its opposition to actions it perceives as interferences in the internal affairs of other states, and it will not assent to peace operations – let alone take part in them – without the agreement of the sovereign host government, however weak its rule may be.[14] Tony Saich (2001, 275) notes, 'By and large, China is an empire with a Westphalian concept of the nation-state trying to operate in an increasingly multilateral world'. This view of sovereignty has arguably often eclipsed China's perception of its responsibilities as a global power. Moreover, it has lay China open to charges of hypocrisy on the subject of non-interference.

For instance, in February 1999, China used its veto to prevent the continuation of the UN Preventive Deployment Force (UNPREDEP) because the host country, Macedonia, had recently established diplomatic relations with Taiwan. Yet in 2004, Beijing dispatched a large contingent of police officers to the US Stabilisation Mission in Haiti (MINUSTAH), which likewise maintained official ties with Taiwan. Such contradictions may be examples of the maturing of Chinese foreign policy.

The Chinese share the prevalent suspicion among developing countries regarding the motives behind potential interventions by foreign powers, especially the United States and ex-colonial powers. Thus they often take the position that, 'in interventions carried out in the name of "humanitarianism" ... what the interveners themselves were concerned about [was] not humanitarianism per se but their own interests' (Qin Xiaocheng 2003, 168). Interestingly, in so doing, they echo Peter Baehr's claim that '"humanitarian intervention" is a misnomer. It would be far better to speak of the use of military force for (allegedly) humanitarian purposes' (Baehr 2004, 34). But such analyses whether by Chinese or Western commentators fail to generate insight into the rationale behind any given intervention. What is required in each case is an investigation into the claims that motivated the intervention and a methodical scrutiny of the endorsement of so-called humanitarianism. Both are sadly lacking.

A Chinese source, quoting a former deputy permanent representative to the UN, Shen Guofang, reminds us of Beijing's central tenet with respect to peacekeeping, namely that it should always observe 'the principles of respect for state sovereignty, non-interference in internal affairs, fairness and neutrality, [and] non-use of force except for self-defence [as well as obtain] prior consent from parties concerned' (*People's Daily,* 21 October 1999). Ambassador Zhang Yishan, at the 2006 Session of the Special Committee on Peacekeeping Operations, reiterated that any UN mission must 'fully respect the views of the parties concerned and strictly preserve neutrality' (*Xinhua,* 27 February 2006). Let us remember that the Chinese government once described the Special Committee for Peacekeeping Operations as an attempt to create 'a US-controlled headquarters of international gendarmes to suppress and stamp out the revolutionary struggles of the world's people' (quoted in Foot 1995, 239). While such rhetoric has been muted in the post-millennium, the suspicion that Washington seeks to use the UN as a vehicle to project its interests and policies is still held by Beijing – and resonates in many African capitals as well.

There are of course tangible rewards for the Chinese military in taking part in peacekeeping operations:

> The PLA and PAP [People's Armed Police] ... directly benefit from involvement in UN peacekeeping operations. First, participation enhances training and skills that promote the modernisation of the PLA and PAP. Second, deployment provides the opportunity to field-test equipment and methods, gain firsthand experience in the field, and assess the capabilities of other nations deploying or supporting the mission. Third, as China's gross domestic product rises, [its] share of UN contributions increases, arguing for greater involvement in operations and greater reimbursement for deployments from UN coffers. (Thompson 2005, 9).

Indeed, speaking at the closing ceremony of the four-day PLA Peacekeeping Work Conference in Beijing in June 2007, Major-General Zhang Qinsheng, Deputy Chief of the general staff of the PLA, revealed that 'active participation in the UN peacekeeping operations is ... an important measure to display China's image of being a peace-loving and responsible big country and likewise an important avenue to get adapted to the needs of the revolution in military affairs in the world and enhance the quality construction of the army' (*PLA Daily*, 22 June 2007). Thus it happily meets a key criterion of Chinese political engagement with Africa – namely that China is seen as a friend of the continent – which means that China's visibility in African peace operations is only likely to grow.

In summary, China's stance on peace operations is intimately bound up with its position on state sovereignty – both of which have, however, evolved over time (Sutter 2008, 117–8). 'China's attitudinal change to peacekeeping can be seen as part of the process of state socialisation .... [P]articipation is an important learning or socialising process [for any] member of an international community. As this learning process continues, we should see a less passive and more active China that needs to craft its own strategies for participation in international affairs in the future' (Pang Zhongying 2005, 98). According to Allen Carlson (2006), 'this process ... aptly labelled "norms diffusion" ... led to the emergence within China of more open, flexible interpretations of sovereignty's role in international politics' (218). However, there are limits to Beijing's flexibility:

> Although China can be flexible in normative principles like state sovereignty and non-intervention ... [it] is aware that its flexibility regarding these norms may be a 'double-edged sword.' On the one hand, when properly used, flexibility can provide Beijing with more diplomatic options for dealing with international affairs, prevent unnecessary conflicts with other powers, and yield a favourable environment for its development strategy. On the other hand, when overexploited, it [does] not only jeopardise China's strategic interests regarding state sovereignty (especially the Taiwan Question) but also damages its image as a peace-loving power, especially in the eyes of the developing world (He Yin 2007, 57).

Paradoxically, the more Beijing becomes enmeshed in global activities, the more it perceives pressures that need to be managed. In fact, it could be argued that Chinese policy toward UN peace operations is largely decided by Beijing's evolving assessment of the global security situation in relation to its national interests as much as by new thinking on sovereignty: 'China's enhanced national strength and its improved status within the international environment provide [the] ... resources and political currency that enable it to adopt an active policy on [UN peace operations]. The aims of such a policy are to sustain its core national interests – including the maintenance of its role as a responsible power, strengthening the UN regime, and sharing common concerns regarding peace and security' (He Yin 2007, 14).

In relation to this, we could argue that Beijing's increasing acceptance of international responsibility as defined by transnational actors like the UN and as reflected in Beijing's emerging status as a contributor to peace operations indicates broader changes in China's political economy. As the Chinese economy becomes more and more integrated into and influenced by the global capitalist system, the CPC is able to identify new, if indirect, sources of political legitimacy. This trend has spurred a 'domestic hunger in China for global linkages [that has] brought down institutional impediments to transnational relations and weakened the state's control over its citizens, resources, and sovereignty' (Zweig 2002, 268).

A peaceful international environment is attractive in this regard. Hu Jintao's concept of *hexie shijie* (*China Daily,* 16 September 2005) is grounded in the recognition that an interdependent, 'harmonious world' is a precondition for China's peaceful development (see Yee Sienho 2008). This new understanding of the international milieu, which relies on flexible definitions of state liability and legitimacy, reflects not only the transformation in Beijing's international relations (Zhao Quansheng 1996) but also that of the Chinese state itself: 'Such thinking serves as a guideline for China's active participation in international efforts and contribution to international peace and security', including UNPKOs (He Yin 2007, 54). While the Chinese remain leery of intervention, they now also accept it as part of the post-Cold War world order. In this sense, 'China is no longer so much of an outlier when compared with other states in the international system' (Carlson 2006, 234). However, this 'cautious acceptance and incremental evolution' in Beijing's attitude toward UNPKOs (Carlson 2006, 224) is a function of Chinese policymakers' attempts to control the terms of intervention, however imprecise they may be. This fact makes the study of Chinese contributions to peace operations on the continent particularly important.

Beijing is resistant to processes whose definitions of sovereignty are out of its control, particularly if they are being shaped by Western powers.[15] As Foot (2001, 14) has pointed out, 'The nature of the international regime in question, especially its level of intrusiveness and the extent to which it might erode strategic independence, threaten political control or actually enhance China's power, has influenced Beijing's compliance and involvement for reasons that have become familiar in studies of Chinese foreign policy behaviour'. In short, Beijing is flexible on sovereignty so long as it is in a position to help define the terms of the debate, but not so long as they are decided by Washington or by a General Assembly vote that it cannot veto. This stance was clear with respect to the Darfur issue.

In other words, the PRC is strongly against the establishment of new norms on such issues. As for international humanitarian law, 'China complies as best it can when it is in its interest to do so but [otherwise] uses whatever techniques at its disposal to resist intrusion into its domestic arena' (Lee 2007, 452). On this score, 'whether China is significantly different ... from other countries is doubtful' (Peerenboom 2005, n. 18).

The reality of Chinese self-interest has important implications not only for China's involvement in peace operations in Africa but also, sometimes unfortunately, for African peoples – Darfurians being the most recent and graphic example. Controlling the terms of the debate on sovereignty in ways that protect Chinese interests remains key to China's stance on intervention and, by extension, peacekeeping. Thus, while China has moved away from absolute repudiation of peace operations to a more responsible point of view that allows limited peace operations, it continues to insist on the express permission of the recipient state or host government.[16] Given the instability of many African states, such insistence is highly problematic and in Sudan certainly delayed the sending of peacekeepers to Darfur long after they were needed.

Yet, responsibility for Africa's domestic conflicts lie more with Africa than with China, a fact that may have an interesting impact on the development of Chinese policies toward sub-Saharan Africa in particular: 'As China becomes involved in volatile regions in its peacekeeping, Beijing will be drawn into conflicts and post-conflict situations and will be forced to think through a coherent policy regarding how such conflicts start and why. This will inevitably have implications for how Beijing regards the make-up of African states'.[17] In summary, we might say that China's attitude toward peace operations has finally been normalised, such that 'the contribution of personnel [to UNPKOs is] more of a routine action ... than an exceptional policy move' (Carlson 2006, 230). How Beijing navigates the African milieu as its involvement in peace operations in Africa deepens will be of great interest to observers of Sino-African relations.

Notes

1. Ian Taylor thanks the Carnegie Trust for the Universities of Scotland, Chiang Ching-kuo Foundation for International Scholarly Exchange, and the Allan and Nesta Ferguson Charitable Trust for their generous support in facilitating extensive fieldwork in Africa, China and elsewhere.
2. Interview with Shu Zhan, Chinese ambassador to Eritrea, Asmara, Eritrea, 29 June 2006.
3. Interview with He Wenping, CASS, Beijing, China, 18 September 2007.
4. Interview with Pentagon official, Washington, DC, United States, 5 April 2007.
5. Interview with Zhou Yuxiao, Chinese ambassador, Monrovia, Liberia, 20 November 2009.
6. Interview with British diplomat, Addis Ababa, Ethiopia, 15 May 2007.
7. Interview with Pentagon official, Washington, DC, United States, 5 April 2007.
8. Interview with Chinese diplomat, Addis Ababa, Ethiopia, 15 May 2007.
9. Interview with Zhou Yuxiao, Chinese ambassador, Monrovia, Liberia, 20 November 2009.
10. Interview with Shu Zhan, Chinese ambassador, Asmara, Eritrea, 29 June 2006.
11. Interview with military attaché, Western embassy, Addis Ababa, Ethiopia, 15 May 2007.
12. Interview with military attaché, Western embassy, Addis Ababa, Ethiopia, 15 May 2007.
13. Interview with Shu Zhan, Chinese ambassador to Eritrea, Asmara, Eritrea, 29 June 2006.
14. Interview with Zhou Yuxiao, Chinese ambassador, Monrovia, Liberia, 20 November 2009.
15. Interview with Shu Zhan, Chinese ambassador to Eritrea, Asmara, Eritrea, 29 June 2006.
16. Interview with Zhou Yuxiao, Chinese ambassador, Monrovia, Liberia, 20 November 2009.
17. Interview with Naison Ngoma, African Union official, Addis Ababa, Ethiopia, 15 May 2007.

Notes on contributors

Wu Zhengyu is an Associate Professor in the School of International Studies, Renmin University of China. His research focuses on Chinese security matters, strategic studies and

International Relations theory. He holds a PhD in International History from Nanjing University. He has previously held visiting scholar positions at the University of Durham, the University of Illinois at Urbana-Champaign, and the London School of Economics and Political Science.

Ian Taylor is a Professor at the University of St. Andrews' School of International Relations and a Joint Professor in the School of International Studies, Renmin University of China, Honorary Professor in the Institute of African Studies, Zhejiang Normal University, China and Professor Extraordinary in Political Science at the University of Stellenbosch, South Africa. Since 1994 he has conducted extensive fieldwork across Africa on China's emerging relationships with the continent.

References

Baehr, P. 2004. Humanitarian intervention: A misnomer. In *International intervention in the post-Cold War world: Moral responsibility and power politics*, ed. M. Davis, W. Dietrich, B. Scholdan, and D. Sepp, 24–35. Armonk, NY: M. E. Sharpe.
Carlson, A. 2004. Helping to keep the peace (albeit reluctantly): China's recent stance on sovereignty and multilateral intervention. *Pacific Affairs* 77, no. 1: 19–26.
Carlson, A. 2006. More than just saying no: China's evolving approach to sovereignty and intervention. In *New Directions in the Study of China's Foreign Policy*, ed. A. Johnston and R. Ross, 217–41. Stanford, CA: Stanford University Press.
Choedon, Y. 2005. China's stand on UN peacekeeping operations: Changing priorities of foreign policy. *China Report* 41, no. 1: 39–57.
Dreyer, J. 2000. *The PLA and the Kosovo conflict*. Carlisle, PA: Strategic Studies Institute.
Elegant, R. 1963. *The centre of the world: Communism and the mind of China*. London: Methuen.
Foot, R. 1995. *The practice of power*. Oxford: Oxford University Press.
Foot, R. 2001. Chinese power and the idea of a responsible state. *China Journal* 45: 19.
Fravel, M.T. 1996. China's attitude toward UN peacekeeping operations since 1989. *Asian Survey* 36, no. 11: 1102–21.
Gill, B. 2007. *Rising star: China's new security diplomacy*. Washington, DC: Brookings Institution Press.
Gill, B., and J. Reilly. 2000. Sovereignty, intervention and peacekeeping: The view from Beijing. *Survival* 42, no. 3: 41–59.
He, W. 2007. The balancing act of China's Africa policy. *China security* 3, no. 3: 23–40.
He, Y. 2007. *China's changing policy on UN peacekeeping operations*. Stockholm: Institute for Security and Development Policy.
Information Office of the State Council. 2002. *White paper on China's national defence*. Beijing: Information Office of the State Council.
James, A. 1993. Internal peace-keeping: A dead end for the UN? *Security Dialogue* 24, no. 4: 359–68.
Kim, S. 1995. China's international organizational behavior. In *Chinese foreign policy: Theory and practice*, ed. T. Robinson and D. Shambaugh, 515–32. Oxford: Oxford University Press.
Lee, K. 2007. China and the international covenant on civil and political rights: Prospects and challenges. *Chinese Journal of International Law* 6, no. 2: 445–74.
Ling, B. 2007. China's peacekeeping diplomacy. *China Rights Forum* 1: 47–9.
Morphet, S. 2000. China as a permanent member of the security council, October 1971–December 1999. *Security Dialogue* 31, no. 2: 151–66.
Pang, Z. 2005. China's changing attitude to UN peacekeeping. *International Peacekeeping* 12, no. 1: 87–104.
Peerenboom, R. 2005. Assessing human rights in China: Why the double standard? *Cornell International Law Journal* 38, no. 1: 71–172.
Qin, X. 2003. Reflections on 'globalization' and state sovereignty. In *International Intervention and State Sovereignty*, 16–24. Beijing: China Reform Forum.
Roy, D. 1998. *China's foreign relations*. London: Macmillan Press.

Saich, T. 2001. *Governance and politics of China*. Basingstoke, UK: Palgrave.
Staehle, S. 2006. China's participation in the United Nations peacekeeping regime. MA thesis, Elliott School of International Affairs, George Washington University.
Sutter, R. 2008. *Chinese foreign relations: Power and policy since the Cold War*. Lanham, MD: Rownan and Littlefield.
Swaine, M. 1995. *China: domestic change and foreign policy*. Santa Monica, CA: RAND.
Thompson, D. 2005. Beijing's participation in UN peacekeeping operations. *Jamestown Foundation China Brief* 5, no. 11: 1–4.
United Nations Security Council. 1997. Security Council establishes UN Observer Mission in Angola (MONUA) mandated to assist Angolan parties to consolidated peace. Press Release SC/6390, 30 June. New York: United Nations.
United Nations Security Council. 1999. Security Council extends Central African Republic Mission Until 15 November. Press Release SC/6651, 26 February. New York: United Nations.
United Nations Secretary-General. 2000. Identical letters dated 21 August 2000 from the Secretary-General to the President of the General Assembly and the President of the Security Council. Press Release A/55/305–S/2000/809. New York: United Nations.
Wang, J. 1999. Managing conflict: Chinese perspectives on multilateral diplomacy and collective security. In *In the eyes of the dragon: China views the world*, ed. Deng Yong and Wang Fei-ling, 73–96. Lanham, MD: Rowman and Littlefield.
Wheeler, N. 2000. *Saving strangers: Humanitarian intervention in international society*. New York: Oxford University Press.
Xia, L. 2001. China: A responsible great power. *Journal of Contemporary China* 10, no. 26: 17–26.
Yee, S. 2008. Towards a harmonious world: The roles of the international law of co-progressiveness and leader states. *Chinese Journal of International Law* 7, no. 1: 99–105.
Zhang, L. 2003. Some reflections on international intervention. In *International Intervention and State Sovereignty*, 26–33. Beijing: China Reform Forum.
Zhang, Y. 1998. *China in international society since 1949: Alienation and beyond*. Oxford: St. Martin's Press.
Zhao, Q. 1996. *Interpreting Chinese foreign policy: The micro-macro linkage approach*. Oxford: Oxford University Press.
Zweig, D. 2002. *Internationalizing China: Domestic interests and global linkages*. Ithaca, NY: Cornell University Press.

The 'voracious dragon', the 'scramble' and the 'honey pot': Conceptions of conflict over Africa's natural resources

Péter Marton and Tamás Matura

Corvinus University of Budapest and Hungarian Institute of International Affairs, Hungary

> Western reactions to China's increasing investment in a number of countries in Africa, as well as Chinese counter-reactions, are often conceptualised as symptoms of a 'honey pot' conflict. Such an impression stems from viewing contemporary African development as a 'new scramble' for the continent's natural resources. However, the study critically unpacks these claims in various fundamental ways, demonstrating how it is untenable. Objections are based on a brief survey of Chinese discourses regarding Western criticism as well empirical objections based on the supposedly 'conflictual' cases of Angola and Sudan, where one in fact finds mutual toleration between the West and China. These realities contradict the assumptions of a honey pot conflict. The study concludes with the alternative proposition that any Sino-Western conflict can be more aptly described as partly self-interest driven, but at the same time normative, and is related to Western concerns about a 'spoiler' role played by China in Africa.

There have in recent years been frequent references to the notion of a 'new scramble for Africa' in popular discourse about the continent's present and future. Indicatively, an article in *The Times*, entitled 'The new scramble for Africa begins', stated that 'Black gangster governments sponsored by self-interested Asian or Western powers could become the central story in twenty-first century African history', warning at the same time that 'modern imperialism on the resource-rich continent will be less benign than old colonialism', and that 'great powers aren't interested in administering wild places any more, still less in settling them: just raping them' (Parris 2008). Such alarmism crosses the political spectrum, with an article in *The Guardian* in 2005 claiming that 'a new "scramble for Africa"' is taking place among the world's big powers, who are tapping into the continent for its oil and diamonds', adding that 'corporations from the US, France, Britain and China are competing to profit from the rulers of often chaotic and corrupt regimes' (Leigh and Pallister 2005). A reflection of such concerns, albeit in a much more sophisticated form, has appeared in scholarly works as well, such as William Reno's seminal *Warlord politics and African states* (1999; see also Lee 2006; Southall and Melber 2009).

An intriguing aspect of the newspaper articles quoted here is the moral equation of 'Western powers' and 'Asian powers', and of the United States, France, Britain and China in the context of contemporary economic relations with Africa. Implicit in this discourse is the proposition their roles are morally highly questionable. At best, the process is deemed unevenly advantageous for Africa, at worst, destructively exploitative.

These concerns are present today in the midst of an economic crisis which once again has led to a re-realisation of the constraints on growth-focused interpretations of development, and the finiteness, if not the already looming scarcity, of many of the vital resources that are needed by wealthier parts of the world to maintain current lifestyles, and which are, at the same time, available from the African continent. The way 'peak oil' and climate change may represent a closely interlinked dual challenge for sustainable development has often been raised in the discourse about emerging global environmental stress (Scott 2008). Consideration of how the near-equivalent of 'peak oil' in ore extraction compounds this challenge is something that should be added to the discussion. The potential depletion of iron, zinc, copper and other mineral reserves beyond what available technology may render extractable is a concern, and adds to the sense of the ongoing 'scramble' for resources. In this context, China's appetite for mineral resources has been dubbed 'insatiable' and 'voracious', and China's shopping list is said to 'run the gamut' of existing minerals, posing a threat to the West (Daly 2008).

This provides a context to the interest in the notion of a 'scramble' in Africa, which implies a zero-sum game for finite resources and one with inherently conflictual dynamics. In such a scramble, gains will inevitably be losses from the other's point of view. The prize is indivisible and impossible to share. Logically, a preference for conflict over cooperation is seemingly a must for players that want to 'win' in this sort of situation. The question that may follow from this is whether there is indeed an ongoing Sino-Western conflict over access to Africa's natural resources, something which media commentators have been assiduous in depicting.

Conflict analysis, shaped to a great extent by contributions from the field of Peace Studies (e.g. Galtung and Jacobsen 2000), focuses on three elements of the conflict triangle to provide a description of the relationship between actors. Incompatibility is ultimately the important element of the triangular scheme: it reflects a perceived or real clash of mutually exclusive interests on the basis of which one can discover the contours of a zero-sum game in the examined relationship. Of course, conflictual situations are also conceivable with more than two players, and alliance formation will not necessarily reduce the number of parties or sides to a clash of interests between two. The 'scramble' for Africa's resources can rather be looked at as a multi-player struggle. Still, out of intellectual laziness perhaps, or out of convenience, taking into account only two sides to a conflict (i.e. 'the West' versus China) does often happen, even in such cases where this may be empirically invalid. Certainly, we often see such portrayals and talk of a Sino-Western conflict in this context.

This is interesting from an abstract point of view. The traditional, partly common-sense-based, partly empirically-verified, working assumption within the literature on armed conflicts has been that natural-resource scarcity – and not an abundance of natural resources – is the likelier cause of conflict. However, by now, even large-N sample quantitative analyses have demonstrated a positive correlation between the abundant presence of natural resources and the probability of the occurrence or re-occurrence of conflict. Several propositions, such as the 'resource curse' hypothesis and the 'honey pot' hypothesis have been formulated to explain why this could be the case in terms of causality (de Soysa 2002; Fournier 2008; Kahl 2002). It is the honey pot hypothesis that is seemingly of more interest when it comes to interpreting the 'scramble' for Africa's resources.

A honey pot is something precious that is worth fighting for. Its role is typically read in two ways in the literature. In its milder form, the honey pot theory suggests that fighting may be sustained by parties to a conflict relying on revenue streams that derive from the control of certain natural resources. In its stronger form, the theory conceives of the honey pot as the actual trigger (not a mere sustaining factor) of violence: as the ultimate incentive explaining the motives of certain actors for their engagement in violent conflict. This reflects the view of the role of natural resources held by Paul Collier and Anke Hoeffler (researchers at the World Bank at the time when they made their mark on the discourse of intra-state armed conflict), to whom the origins of the discussion of 'honey pots' is most often attributed (Collier 2000; Collier and Hoeffler 1998). Their research has had an unintended negative influence on the analysis of contemporary conflict, fuelling the 'new war' discourse, which suggests that today's conflicts are, in general, markedly different from the conflicts of the past. This interpretation sees today's supposedly 'different' conflicts as being motivated primarily by greed instead of grievance, enjoying no mass, popular support and engaging in predominantly 'random' violence, instead of the highly selective use of force that supposedly characterised war in the past. Though Collier and Hoeffler did not apparently intend to suggest that grievances do not matter any more, their focus on greed-based explanations has been seized on to take a view that essentially criminalises contemporary rebellions (see critical thoughts on this by Kalyvas 2001). We can see in this a form of 'IGO statism' as present in, and partly explaining, the emergence of, this philosophy (i.e. a general preference by states in multilateral organisations such as the United Nations (UN) and the World Bank who cannot – or will not – deal with rebel movements as having any legitimacy). They thus run into major hurdles in conflict-torn countries in the course of trying to fulfil institutional missions (Marton 2008, 99).

The discursive implications of the appearance of the honey pot concept has been a somewhat artificial (and thus superficial) debate on whether abundance rather than scarcity is the *more likely* cause of natural resources contributing to conflict, and a debate over the varying impacts of different natural resources on conflict. As persuasively demonstrated by Kahl (2002) and Fournier (2008), the first debate presented a false dilemma, as in fact the local abundance of a natural resource may be inflated in value by increasing global scarcity of the same resource and also local fighting over a locally abundant natural resource may arise as the indirect outcome of local scarcities with regards to *other* key natural resources in the given area. The second debate about the impact of resources on conflict received important input from Kahl (2002), who pointed out bias in that the abundance-focused theories were, implicitly, focusing on non-renewable resources that can indeed easily serve as honey pots, unlike renewable resources. Other authors, such as Le Billon (2001, 570) presented conflict-sensitive typologies of natural resources showing how different the conflict impact of natural resources (possible honey pots) can be, depending on whether they are proximate to the capital or in an outlying region; point-source or diffuse (spread over a larger area); lootable or not; obstructible or not; or legal or illegal.

These contributions have all been tremendously valuable, but the discourse has become skewed in the sense that it has left a key potential of the honey pot concept untapped: namely the possibility of interpreting it as an explaining factor not just in terms of intra-state armed conflict, but in interstate conflict as well. This is despite the fact that one is likely to find Marxist authors sympathetic to taking this seriously as a factor driving conflict between capitalist states. Intriguingly, a great many of what Wallensteen (2007) refers to as cases of 'Geopolitik' and 'Kapitalpolitik' conflicts (106) in fact can be seen as taking place over the material control of, or access to, honey pots.

Beyond this potential appeal of the concept, the absence of reading honey pots into interstate contexts is puzzling for two more basic reasons. One concerns empirical reality, surely a key underlying assumptions of theory. Firstly, there are some outstanding empirical examples of key natural resources playing the role of a honey pot in interstate conflict in history. For one, the example of the Rumailah oil fields could perhaps suffice in showing how rights to oil extraction in these fields and accusations of slant-drilling contributed to the rise of tensions between Iraq and Kuwait. These tensions were certainly not the only source of the eventual, rather one-sided armed confrontation between the two countries in 1990 but it is, in fact, no problem for conflict analysis to take into account, parallel to each other, more than just one incompatibility defining the relationship between two actors. Secondly, a key criticism (Kahl 2006) of the strong version of the honey pot hypothesis is that the presence of a honey pot cannot, as an acting agent could, take care of the organisation of a capable fighting party that can challenge the rule of an incumbent regime over a natural resource. This is relevant, as in interstate relations the existence of more or less capable actors is already a given in the context where a valuable honey pot may come to be identified. Thus here the honey pot hypothesis may be regarded as *more* valid, at least in this particular sense.

This could be food for thought for research into a number of interesting cases. In this study the question we are putting forward with all the considerations hitherto outlined is whether Western criticism of China's increasing investment in Africa, or, parallel to this, criticisms of a Sino-Western 'scramble' for economic opportunities in Africa, could be viewed as the correct perception of an interstate honey pot conflict (i.e. a conflict over Africa's increasingly valuable natural resources, between an alliance of Western and other states, and the emerging power that is China).

As referred to before, on the basis of this one could gain a seemingly convenient conflict analysis framework. To this, however, the world would then need to fit, obediently. But this may not fit in reality. This study thus examines and critically weakens the assumption of a West vs. China honey pot conflict from a number of aspects. Firstly, conceptually, by problematising the interpretations of 'sides' to any notional conflict, the territorial and the structural delimitation of the 'honey pot' and the notion of 'conflict behaviour' (and the question of whether conflict behaviour occurs at all). Secondly, the study looks at Chinese discourses and attempts to gauge whether these fit the picture of a Sino-Western honey pot conflict, in terms of observable and/or demonstrated attitudes. Thirdly, it looks at empirical examples of less than unambiguous cases of confrontation between Western and Chinese policies towards two African countries, which buttresses our criticism of the honey pot assumption.

Conceptual objections

The primary objection that can be raised conceptually is that while the honey pot assumption effectively posits that there are two sides to a conflict fighting for their own gains, in the context of the geo-politico-economics of African natural resources we cannot clearly identify such a clash. Indeed, an important (counter-)argument against the talk of opposing sides when it comes to extracting Africa's oil for instance, concerns the wrongly assumed unitary-actor or monolithic character of 'the Chinese'. In fact, Beijing inevitably and increasingly faces difficulties in executing any coordinated strategy due to the complexity of its bureaucracy and the behaviour of its state-owned enterprises (SOEs). This plays out in the form of the oft-seen phenomenon of the principal agent problem. Coordination is already lacking (Downs 2007, 48–51). The supposedly monolithic Chinese repeatedly experience competition between Chinese SOEs on the one hand and weak coordination between its Ministry of Foreign Affairs and the parastatals on the other. At the same time, 'the West' obviously should be broken up into various actors, given their not entirely convergent policies both at the state and corporate level.

A second conceptual objection concerns the territorial delimitation of the honey pot. This objection does not concern the spatial attributes of the African natural resources concerned (i.e. the question of whether these are point-source or diffuse). Rather, territorial delimitation concerns the larger question of whether conflict between China and the West could possibly be taking place *purely* over African resources, as these resources are also found elsewhere. Referring back to the introductory discussion we mentioned that one of the most important criticisms regarding whether honey pot conflicts are caused by an abundance of natural resources is whether local relative abundance might in fact stem from global scarcity. The latter, in turn, is the outcome of the dynamic interplay of global demand and supply. No source of global supply could be ignored in a consistent analysis, therefore.

For instance, there has been growing interest, and in some circles concern, regarding China's investments in Latin America, for example in Peruvian copper-mining, which has been typically cast by *The Economist* as 'The dragon in the backyard'. In American circles there are worries about the unmaking of the mutual dependence in US–Venezuelan relations, which stems from American refining capabilities specifically adapted to Venezuela's heavy and sulphurous crude oil. Meanwhile, some American scholars assert that China is not courting 'the Left' in Latin America, but that rather China has no interests other than diplomacy, trade and investment. In this light, 'the expanding role of China in Latin America should be viewed as a singular opportunity to strengthen all three relationships in the Sino-US-Latin American triangle' (Roett and Paz 2008, 19–20).

Based on all this, any honey pot should rather be defined as the *global* pool of increasingly scarce natural resources. There could arguably be conflict over this wider pool, not only in Africa but across the globe, between Western countries and China.

However, based on the next key consideration we outline here, we argue that one needs to reconsider this view.

This, our third conceptual objection, concerns the sectoral delimitation of the honey pot. As Gawdat Bahgat notes:

> Current and projected characteristics of global oil markets indicate a strong need for close cooperation between producers, consumers and international oil companies. Such cooperation would underscore the common interests all these parties share. It would also ensure both the security of supplies and demand. In short, close cooperation between all major players in the oil industry would contribute to overall stability of global oil markets and international economy (Bahgat 2007, 94).

Specifically with regards to the African context, Bahgat adds, 'the competition between Washington, Beijing and Brussels over Africa's energy resources should not be seen in zero-sum terms. The underlying and inescapable fact is that the development of the continent's oil resources would contribute to overall stability in global oil markets – a shared goal by both consumers and producers' (ibid., 101). Bahgat talks about a need for oil producers and consumers to work in 'constructive interdependence', something that would probably not afford the conclusion that short-term opportunity (and pay-off) structures fully discourage conflictual strategies on the part of individual consuming or producing countries and the corporations involved. But it certainly appears so that more cooperation among consumers and producers, even if it comes with disagreements over human rights and other issues, is rewarded by current structural conditions.

To underscore the importance of how much interdependence and potential mutual benefit there is for consumers in opening up access to African resources, Downs points out how in 2006 China's China National Petroleum Corporation (CNPC) sold most of its Sudanese oil production on the international market, rather than to Chinese buyers (Downs 2007, 47–8). Others have pointed out that critics should realise that China is not somehow taking oil off the market. Moreover, the supply of oil, natural gas, ores, etc feed value supply chains of global production. Given this, talk of conflict over supposedly isolated honey pots, of value in and of themselves, makes no sense. It would disregard structural interdependence at levels further up value chains.

Finally, one can also raise objections to the honey pot assumption based on a simple, formal conflict assessment of Sino-Western relations. A restrictive interpretation of conflict does not leave much to be assessed in the sub-Saharan African context. There is in fact no actual fighting, or direct violence, taking place between the parties concerned. Nevertheless this is not too strong a counter-argument. Galtung's Peace Studies approach emphasises the possibility of structural conflicts over incompatibilities of interests (see, for example, Galtung 1996). That is just what the concept of the interstate honey pot conflict mostly entails in the context we are examining: it is a structural explanation of the *discursive* phenomenon of Western criticism with regards to China's role in Africa, and other criticisms regarding a 'scramble' in Sino-Western relations. Nevertheless one does not even find an unambiguous case of Sino-Western proxy warfare on the continent.

What may remain to be analysed therefore, to test the honey pot assumption further (and to decisively reject it), is whether the discourse might still show the influence of the notion of a Sino-Western honey pot conflict; and whether in concrete cases one might find behaviour from the parties concerned that might correspond to what one could expect in a structural (i.e. not directly/overtly violent) honey pot conflict?

Objections based on discourse analysis

The following section of the study proceeds to briefly survey Chinese discourses about Sino-African relations, based on works by Chinese authors. English language sources are studied for this purpose – not out of convenience but because these are the sources that are self-evidently *made available* in the sense of being better-accessible to the outside world and which contribute to a wider global discourse. This is a valuable effort for two reasons. One is that studying Chinese discourses can offer further counter-arguments to any Western notion of a Chinese threat (and thus to the notion of a Sino-Western conflict). The other, paradoxically, is that any sign of a Chinese discursive response to Western criticism could reflect Chinese concern about the impact of Western criticism and Chinese perceptions so that it therefore needs to be addressed. The latter finding would not, in and of itself, verify that there is a structural honey pot conflict in Sino-Western relations, but it could be sign of how important protecting access to these natural resources is to China.

Reviewing the Chinese side one can find that, contrary to divergent Western discourses, in the People's Republic of China the academic and official sources mainly sing in unison. Most of the sources convey an impression that Beijing's behaviour aims to avoid engaging in open diplomatic or strategic confrontation with the US and the EU in Africa. In general, Chinese papers evade directly responding to points of Western criticism, but their argumentation consistently follows Western condemnation. It is seen as China's vital interest to push for multi-polarity in world politics and to ensure a reliable supply of natural resources from Africa supporting its own development (Cheng and Shi 2009). The most important Chinese academic institutes of international affairs are providing argumentation *in conjunction* with governmental responses to Western criticism of China's expansion in Africa, or the so-called 'China threat in Africa' theory (regarding this term see Zong He 2007).

There are several recurring elements in the Chinese discourse. Papers and official documents emphasise the friendly and mutually beneficial relations between Beijing and African countries, without – unsurprisingly – mentioning any tensions or problems in these relations. The crucial Chinese policy document about the continent, i.e. China's African Policy (CAP 2006), contains almost every aspect of Beijing's official view of Sino-African relations. The document sets out the general principles and objectives of China's Africa policy as sincerity, friendship and equality, the Five Principles of Peaceful Coexistence (*heping gongchu wuxiang yuanze* or Panchsheel), mutual benefit, mutual support, and close coordination. Thought to share similar experiences given the long-time influence in its affairs of Western powers, China and Africa have all along supposedly sympathised with and supported each other in the struggle for national liberation and forged a profound friendship.

Elements of these sentiments can be found in all other Chinese papers concerning the role of the PRC in Africa and Western reactions. Key elements of the Chinese argumentation defending China's positions in Africa are the aid programmes funded by Beijing to support African countries, centred on the idea of 'non-political conditionality', and bolstered by a corresponding theoretical framework. According to the substantive element of 'non-political conditionality', China respects the sovereignty of African countries, and does not intervene in their domestic affairs, noting that these are principles enshrined in the UN Charter (Zhang Zhongxiang 2008, 44).

The UN is an important reference point in Chinese discourses, since multipolarity plays a significant role in dominant Chinese thinking about international relations theory and foreign policy making. In this discourse, Beijing has been on generally good terms with the UN at least since 25 October 1971, when the General Assembly adopted Resolution 2758, recognising the PRC as the sole legal government of China. Among the 76 supporting votes on the occasion, 26 were from African countries (Zhang Yunfei 2007). 'It is our African brothers who carried us into the United Nations', as Mao Zedong once said.

Regarding human rights cooperation, a paper by Hong Kong-based researchers Joseph Cheng and Shi Huangao (2009) presents arguably more independent analysis. Cheng and Shi provide tables about African countries' voting record on no action motions concerning the condemnation of the human rights situation in China. According to the data they provide, it is evident that African countries are great supporters of Chinese political interests. Between 1990 and 2004, on average, 46.6% of supporting votes were African, and only 5.1% of African votes were supportive of any condemnation of China. In light of this, one may realise that there are aspects to Sino-African relations that typically receive disproportionately scarce attention from a West-centric point of view, while they clearly matter a great deal from a Beijing perspective.

Western criticism is rarely addressed directly in Chinese discourse, albeit one may implicitly see a defensive reaction in how articles tend to emphasise only the positive aspects of Sino-African relations. A remarkable exception is an article by Zong He (2007) in response to what Zong calls the Western 'theory' of the 'China threat in Africa'. In this argumentation Zong builds on almost every recurring element and underlying assumption of the dominant Chinese discourse about Africa, writing that the theory of this threat has been played up by Western media as part of the more general notion of the 'China threat'. Zong sets out four Western allegations in particular, which are completely false in his point of view. Firstly, that the West suggests that China has been pursuing 'neo-colonialism' in Africa, using cooperation to plunder Africa's natural resources. Instead, China and Africa are, as Zong asserts, 'friends and partners', with a partnership based on sincerity, equality, trust and friendship. Zong points out that China takes only 10% of Africa's total export of crude oil, while the US and Europe take 69% together. Secondly, Zong reacts to Western criticism of China's position of non-interference in other countries' internal affairs, and its relations with some 'problematic' countries, condemning Western attitudes about the supposed need to attach strings to assistance, contrary to Chinese aid policy that respects the independent development path of every African country. The third point of Western accusations in Zong's summary is that China pursues mercantilism and profit in Africa. In his view, however, the true nature of the Chinese approach is better reflected in the generous assistance it provides in the field of developing Africa's infrastructure, agriculture, medical care, education, and in its contributions to social development in African countries. According to Zong, China's trade with Africa contributes about 20 percent of its economic growth, and that is why African countries see China's development as an opportunity, and not as a threat. The fourth and final topic Zong raises is that of China's preferential loans to Africa. The West alleges that these loans are almost free and that they are undermining the potentially beneficial impact of debt relief efforts of the West. Zong's opinion is that these soft loans were mainly used in improving infrastructure, importing machinery and building manufacturing enterprises in Africa. Furthermore, China has also cancelled renminbi (RMB) 11 billion worth of debt for 31 heavily indebted poor and least developed countries (HIPCs and LDCs) in Africa. The conclusion of the essay is therefore that the assertion of a 'China threat' in Africa cannot stand (Zong He 2007).

Based on the overview hitherto outlined, we see grounds for cautiously concluding that while there does seem to be some partly emotional, partly interest-based concern in Chinese circles about Western criticism of China's record in African countries, the opposition put up in reaction to this seems to be mostly about genuinely argued points of counter-criticism. The discursive reaction reflects less a concern about the West grabbing hold of greater gains in the zero-sum game of a 'scramble' for the African honey pot, and more an emotional, moralising, but at the same time reasoning, objection to accusations and criticisms considered by Beijing to be unjust.

Empirical objections: A few observations

Should there be a zero-sum game or a honey pot conflict over Africa's natural resources between the West and China or an irrational notion of such conflict informing the practice of the key actors, one should not find much mutual toleration in the practices of those countries concerned on the ground, particularly in countries where such a conflict could play out. Yet a cursory overview of the supposedly 'conflictual' Angolan and Sudanese cases reveals that even in these cases one can observe mutual toleration by the parties.

Angola is one of the countries with which China is deepening cooperation related to its oil imports, along with the Republic of Congo, Gabon, Equatorial Guinea, Sudan and Nigeria. Keenan described China's outreach to the country as generally disincentivising reform and derailing Western attempts at putting pressure on the Angolan government for more transparency. To underscore this, he cited Chinese readiness to provide what essentially amounted to 'replacement loans' to the country at a time, in 2004, when the International Monetary Fund (IMF) was demanding better governance as a condition for its assistance. These calls were made in the wake of allegations that approximately $4 billion in oil revenues had gone 'missing', probably embezzled by Angolan elite circles. This may have been just the tip of the iceberg in a country that made $30 billion from oil exports in 2006 alone, with oil revenues amounting to 93% of export earnings, 78% of government revenues and 52% of GDP (Keenan 2009, 98–100). Keenan argues, however, that even well-intentioned, conditionality-based assistance could have a corrupting effect, and that thus one would not necessarily see much better governance outcomes in the absence of the availability of Chinese resources to these countries (Keenan 2009).

Moreover, demands for conditionality notwithstanding, Western countries and corporations are just as eager to do business with Angola as others. Hanson quotes David Kang as saying that 'the United States is highly selective about who we're moral about' (Hanson 2008, 24). Angolan President dos Santos' regime may be (rightly) criticised for its handling of human rights or for the rampant poverty that stands in contrast to the abundance of natural resources it is making profits from, but its American and other Western business partners at this point seem comfortable working with this and being part of the system that perpetuates it. Angolan oil accounts for up to 7% of US import needs, and this figure seems set to rise, while new investment also arrives to the country to start up the exportation of liquified natural gas.

Mutual toleration in this single (albeit important) case may still leave room for more conflictual approaches elsewhere. That is why a brief overview of the Sudanese context follows, given the extent to which there has been much criticism in Western discourse regarding China's Sudan policy. In an excellent case study, Patey (2007) outlined how a simple narrative of Western oil companies gradually leaving as a result of public pressure over human rights concerns, to have their place taken by Chinese parastatals, cannot stand up to a scrutiny of the facts. He examined how Chevron downsized its involvement in the country as a result of violent incidents near or against its facilities, American government concerns over Sudan's support to terrorist organisations at the time, and Washington DC's push to move into former Soviet spheres of influence in the promising Caucasian, Caspian and Central Asian regions, at the end of the Cold War. This, at the same time, did not mean the end of Western (i.e. Canadian or EU-based) companies' involvement in the Sudan. In fact it opened up room for European companies that had a more permissive political context for making their investments, given for example the EU's Sudan policy of 'constructive engagement'. The EU-based companies' involvement shows how telling this complex story is from the angle of a 'Sino-Western clash' and how this story is not workable. In the second half of the 1990s, not only Chinese, but also Indian, Malaysian and other companies made major investments in the Sudan *alongside* their Western counterparts.

Most notably perhaps, when the United States introduced a new round of economic sanctions against Sudan in 2007, related to the conflict in Darfur, not only did these sanctions not have the EU's unanimous support (destabilising the notion of 'the West') but they also did *not* target the CNPC (Gerstenzang and Sanders 2007). This is not to say that CNPC has not seen any repercussions from American activists' mobilisation against their involvement in the Sudan, for example in raising capital on the US financial market (Patey 2007, 1011), but it has received velvet-gloved treatment from the American administration that has appeared just as careful not to antagonise China, in this case, as the Chinese leadership appears, in general, to avoid a direct strategic confrontation with Western interests and endeavours. This is hardly what one should find if the honey pot assumption with a China versus 'the West' scenario was valid.

Conclusion

Based on this rudimentary overview of objections to explaining the Sino-Western discursive exchange of arguments and counter-arguments as a honey pot conflict, we conclude that the real underlying conflict is primarily normative. Our alternative thesis, in regard of which further inquiry may be needed beyond studies already available, is that this is a management or norm-contestation conflict between stakeholders in global governance, between countries with important influence in the world economy and thus in a position to set the course and the norms of this global governance. The intangible good of control over the latter is more the object of conflict rather than Africa's natural resources. Some may refer to this as a clash between the Washington Consensus and the alternative 'Beijing Consensus' (Halper 2010), though we have doubts about the coherence of the latter. Indeed, it is noteworthy that the term was coined *outside* China. Beijing does not wish to comprehensively and openly challenge the West's ideational hegemony. Yet correspondingly, the West is concerned by the 'spoiler' role China is often claimed to be playing.

'The West', united in name only, is looking to preserve its dominant voice in post-colonial Africa's affairs with reference to arguably mutually beneficial norms of governance, even while practicing self-interest-based selectivity in applying these very norms in a number of cases. Paradoxically, some of the mentioned selectivity is dressed in equally normative terms, for example when engaging condemned regimes is deemed 'constructive' (e.g. Sudan). China, on the other hand, *seems* to be more consistent in its tolerant approach, respectful of the sovereignty of its partners, but clearly this is also rooted in the pursuit of self-interest.

A zero-sum game over access to African natural resources is *not* taking place at the moment, as Africa is more than capable of satisfying the growing demands for its resources from the parties concerned. This does not exclude the possibility of a future honey pot conflict, should resources become globally increasingly scarce, economies much more closed at some point, or Sino-Western relations more tense than they are currently today – although given the extensive interdependency of the global economy this would be disastrous for *all* sides and hence unlikely. For now, however, viewing the African encounter of Chinese and Western endeavours through the lens of a honey pot conflict remains merely an intellectual game and one that is not accurate and devoid of empirical relevance or evidence.

As to the use of the honey pot concept in the analysis of interstate conflict, the safest conclusion one can draw is that new analytical categories ought to be conceptualised, and further hypotheses and theories developed. This is necessary to better identify possible variations of what impact natural resources can have on interstate conflict. To refer back to the seemingly more useful example of the Rumailah oil fields, in that case at issue were rights over a transnationally located oil field that could have been controlled or extracted (e.g. through slant-drilling) in its entirety by one of the opposing parties. One cannot simplistically claim with plausibility that any other kind of natural resource, in any location, will similarly lead to conflict between any pair of neighbouring states.

Note on contributors

Péter Marton is adjunct and research fellow at the Corvinus University of Budapest. He has in the past worked for the Hungarian Institute of International Affairs. His research focuses on the transnational aspects of conflict and state-building in Africa.

Tamás Matura is a research fellow of the Hungarian Institute of International Affairs, and a doctoral student of the International Relations Doctoral School at the Corvinus University of Budapest. His research deals mainly with China's foreign policy and its international relations.

References

Bahgat, G. 2007. Africa's oil: Potential and implications. *OPEC Review* March: 1–7.
CAP. 2006. *China's African policy*. Beijing: Ministry of Foreign Affairs.
Cheng, J., and Shi Huangao. 2009. China's African policy in the post-Cold War era. *Journal of Contemporary Asia* 39: 89–115.
Collier, P. 2000. Rebellion as a quasi-criminal activity. *Journal of Conflict Resolution* 44: 839–53.
Collier, P., and A. Hoeffler. 1998. On the economic causes of civil war. *Oxford Economic Papers*, 50: 563–73.
Daly, J. 2008. Feeding the dragon: China's quest for African minerals. *China Brief*, 8: 3.
De Soysa, I. 2002. Ecoviolence: Shrinking pie, or honey pot? *Global Environmental Politics* 2: 1–34.
Downs, E. 2007. The fact and fiction of Sino-African energy relations. *China Security* 3: 42–68.
Fournier, J.-B. 2008. In the wilderness with a honey pot and a shrinking pie: An overview of the ecoviolence debate. *Undercurrent Journal* 5: 14–20.
Galtung, J. 1996. *Peace by peaceful means: Peace and conflict, development and civilization*. London: Sage.
Galtung, J., and C. Jacobsen. 2000. *Searching for peace: The road to TRANSCEND*. London: Pluto Press.
Gerstenzang, J., and E. Sanders. 2007. Bush action on Sudan is limited. *Los Angeles Times*, 30 May.
Halper, S. 2010. *The Beijing consensus: How China's Authoritarian model will dominate the twenty-first century*. New York: Basic Books.
Hanson, S. 2008. *China, Africa, and oil*. New York: Council on Foreign Relations.
Kahl, C.H. 2002. Demographic change, natural resources and violence: The current debate. *Journal of International Affairs* 56: 257–82.
Kahl, C. 2006. *States, scarcity, and civil strife in the developing world*. Princeton: Princeton University Press.
Kalyvas, S.N. 2001. 'New' and 'old' civil wars: A valid distinction? *World Politics* 54: 98–115.
Keenan, P. 2009. Curse or cure? China, Africa, and the effects of unconditioned wealth. *Berkeley Journal of International Law* 27: 17–31.
Le Billon, P. 2001. The political ecology of war: Natural resources and armed conflicts. *Political Geography* 20: 561–84.
Lee, M. 2006. The 21st century scramble for Africa. *Journal of Contemporary African Studies* 24: 303–40.
Leigh, D., and D. Pallister. 2005. Revealed: The new scramble for Africa. *The Guardian*, 1 June.
Marton, P. 2008. Global governance vs. state failure. *Perspectives: Central European Review of International Affairs* 16: 85–107.
Parris, M. 2008. The new scramble for Africa begins. *The Times*, 19 April.
Patey, L.A. 2007. State rules: Oil companies and armed conflict in Sudan. *Third World Quarterly* 28: 997–1016.
Reno, W. 1999. *Warlord politics and African states*. Boulder, Colorado: Lynne Rienner.
Roett, R. and Paz, G., eds. 2008. *China's expansion into the western hemisphere: Implications for Latin America and the United States*. Washington, D.C: Brookings Institution.
Scott, S.V. 2008. Climate change and peak oil as threats to international peace and security: Is it time for the security council to legislate? *Melbourne Journal of International Law* 9: 495–514.
Southall, R. and Melber H., eds. 2009. *A new scramble for Africa? Imperialism, investment and development*. Pietermartizburg: University of Kwazulu-Natal Press.
Wallensteen, P. 2007. *Understanding conflict resolution: War, peace and the global system*. London: Sage Publications.
Zhang, Y. 2007. China-Africa cooperation within the framework of the United Nations. *Foreign Affairs Journal* 83: 67–75.

Zhang, Z. 2008. China's model of aiding Africa and its implications. *International Review*, 41: 41–54.
Zong, H. 2007. Some observations in response to 'China threat in Africa'. *China Daily*, 7 November.

Uneasy allies: China's evolving relations with Angola

Lucy Corkin

School of Oriental and African Studies, University of London, London, UK

> By conventional accounts, following the so-called 'Angola Model', the Chinese government is heavily involved in the national reconstruction programme through various financial institutions as a means to ensure closer relations with Angola and thus access to oil. China's strategy is thus ostensibly to accumulate political capital through the provision of infrastructure, financed by oil-backed concessional loans extended by Chinese state-owned banks. This study briefly traces the history of China's relations with Angola before examining the various parallel structures involved in the two country's co-operation over infrastructure, loans and oil. It examines the so-called 'Angola Model' by looking at three key assumptions surrounding risk, access to oil and China's political access in Angola. The study also evaluates the nature of the so-called 'strategic partnership' for both Angola and China. Political posturing indicates that both China and Angola see each other as necessary strategic allies for the foreseeable future, but this may mask an uneasy marriage of convenience.

China's role in Angola as a financier of large-scale development projects has received considerable media attention, but relations, both historical and contemporary, have as yet received limited scholarly attention (Taylor 2006). Angola achieved independence in 1975 and only established official diplomatic ties with China in 1983. Consequently, Angola's official bilateral contact with China does not boast as long a history as that of other African states. In this so-called new type of China–Africa strategic partnership, China has only been a serious actor in Angola since 2004 (Corkin 2008b, 110). This does not mean, however, that interaction did not occur before official diplomatic ties were established. China had extensive involvement in Angola's protracted civil war. Indeed, the late development of official diplomatic relations could be attributed to China's disastrous participation in Angola's internal conflict. Both the Soviet-backed Movimento Popular para a Libertação de Angola (MPLA) and the União Nacional para a Independência Total de Angola (UNITA), as well as several other liberation movements received support from China, as described by Taylor (2006). Snow (1988, 77) draws attention to the fact that despite China's initial support of UNITA, the MPLA's first crucial, albeit limited, funding came from China. The MPLA leadership actually experienced a schism as to whether to ally with the Soviet Union or China. Viriato da Cruz, one of the founding fathers of the MPLA, was ousted as a result of the decision to follow Moscow, fleeing to Beijing, where he died in exile. It is suspected that the liberation movement turned to the Soviets in order to access more advanced weapons technology than those available from China.

Taylor (2006, 81) places some importance on China's earlier role in Angola, as support of UNITA in an unwitting alliance with apartheid South Africa (and 'imperialist' USA), cost China dearly in diplomatic terms. Desphande and Gupta (1986, 46) concur that China's early intervention in Angola was calamitous for China's relations with African countries. Apart from violating China's sacrosanct principle of non-interference, China's de facto alliance with apartheid South Africa drew heavy criticism from even China's closest allies on the continent. Such foreign policy failures on the part of China were precipitated by ideological overreach and a miscalculation of the complexity of the African context. This historical background may have provided added impetus to the Chinese government's willingness to reach an economic agreement in favour of Angola years later, in order to compensate for China's messy involvement in Angola's civil war.[1]

The turn of the century, however, marked a new phase of bilateral interaction, focusing on increasingly economically driven and pragmatic relations (Campos and Vines 2007; Corkin 2008b), particularly as regards Angola's plans for post-war reconstruction (Burke and Corkin 2006). Angola is currently China's largest African trading partner, primarily due to China's hunger for crude oil, and currently more than 30% of Angola's crude exports go to China, accounting for 16% of China's total oil imports (Stratfor 2009). Indeed, the ruling party now has strong ties to Beijing due to China Exim Bank's and several other Chinese financial institutions' sizeable loans to the Angolan government (Taylor 2009).

Investigating the 'Angola Model'

The 'Angola Model' is so named due to its initial emergence in Angola and is shorthand for a supposed method of financing preferred by the Chinese government whereby funds, usually for infrastructural development in African countries, are secured using natural resources as collateral. Having first appeared briefly in several publications (Chen *et al.* 2007; Burke *et al.* 2007; Corkin 2007a, 2007b), the concept received a more in-depth investigation from a World Bank report in 2008 (Foster *et al.* 2008).

However, there is little that is unique about the so-called 'Angola Model', given that it is not the first time that Angola has secured oil-backed financing to support large-scale infrastructure projects (Corkin 2008a, 182; Vines *et al.* 2009, 47). It is in this light that the 'Angola Model' requires further investigation. To this end, this study seeks to investigate three widely held assumptions regarding the China Exim Bank's involvement in Angola: firstly as a policy bank, the Bank has no regard for commercial risk; secondly that the loans were extended to Angola in order to access oil equity; and thirdly, China's involvement in Angola accords China preferential status as a trade and investment partner.

China Exim Bank enters Angola

After the death of Jonas Savimbi and the collapse of UNITA resistance in 2002, the MPLA government was desperate to access funding to rebuild the country after the civil war. The end of the Cold War had lost Angola its earlier strategic significance, resulting in a lack of interest by the parties that had previously been so involved in

Angola's political landscape. The International Monetary Fund (IMF), while prepared to offer loans, was insistent on increased transparency and a macro-economic stabilisation policy, aimed at reducing inflation by cutting public expenditure. Consequently, any large-scale infrastructure reconstruction programme funded by the IMF would have to wait until Angola had achieved a healthier fiscal situation. These conditions were not acceptable to the Angolan elites however, thus President dos Santos appealed to China.[2] Negotiations began in 2003 and the first loan agreement with the China Exim Bank came into effect on 21 March 2004. Between 2004–2007, China's Exim Bank extended a total of $4.5 billion in oil-backed credit lines to the Angolan government – An additional China Exim Bank credit line of US$ 6 billion was announced in July 2010.[3]

The loans extended by China Exim Bank are targeted specifically towards facilitating public investment in Angola and are reportedly managed by the Angolan Ministry of Finance (Burke *et al.* 2007; Vines *et al.* 2009). According to the terms of the loans, Chinese companies are largely contracted to undertake required projects and are paid directly by China Exim Bank, which writes down the contract amount against the loan available to the Angolan government. The loan is repayable at Libor[4] plus 1.5% over 17 years, including a grace period of five years.[5] These terms render a less expensive financing option than the oil-backed loans extended to the Angolan government by previous financiers.

Accepting loans from China was politically expedient for the Angolan political elite on two counts. Firstly, Angola had been experiencing difficulties securing other sources of capital on conditions acceptable to the state regime. Furthermore, with an eye on the inevitability of national and presidential elections, the ruling party saw the political dividends of public investment in infrastructure.[6]

Tied to the China Exim Bank loan is the agreement that the public tenders, for the construction and civil engineering contracts tabled for Angola's reconstruction, will be awarded primarily (70%) to Chinese enterprises approved by Beijing. Of the remaining tenders, 30% have reportedly been allocated to the Angolan private sector, to encourage Angolan participation in the reconstruction process (Corkin 2008c) although this may only extend as far as ensuring that 30% of contracted labour is Angolan.[7] Up to 60% of tenders awarded to Chinese companies may also be subcontracted to local partners. Each project must be valued to be at least $10 million.

While an impressive array of infrastructure has been completed since 2004, the execution of these projects has not been without its challenges. The main hurdles are bureaucratic capacity, poor understanding of the operating environment on the part of the Chinese companies and supply bottlenecks (Corkin 2008a). This is unlikely to improve in the short-term, although it is expected that contracted Chinese companies will learn to be less ambitious in setting their planned project completion targets. There are also fears that the massive infrastructural spending planned by the government will be misdirected if it is not complemented by capacity-building and training programmes to improve Angola's ability to absorb investment of such a magnitude. The problem is compounded by the fact that due to a lack of local capacity and short supply, most construction materials and often the technical construction expertise need to be imported (Burke and Corkin 2007, 37).

Parallel structures of Chinese financing in Angola

What is perhaps unique in Angola's situation is the presence of two seemingly parallel and unrelated financing structures directed from China to Angola. Beneath the smooth rhetoric of 'win-win' co-operation, Angola's relations with China have been fraught at times. It has also been complicated by the entry into Angola of various Chinese financial institutions, whose links to the Chinese government are often ill-defined.[8] Additional loans from the China International Fund Ltd (CIF), a Hong Kong-based company, have been placed under the auspices of Gabinete de Reconstrução Nacional (GRN), headed by General Helder Vieira Dias 'Kopelipa', who is also Minister in Chief of the Presidency. The GRN was created specifically to manage credit lines from CIF. GRN is an instrument of the executive, as are the various other *gabinetes*. The loans managed by GRN are estimated to be in excess of $9 billion.[9] However, according to a press release issued by the Angolan state in response to the controversy surrounding the circumstances of these loans, the actual loan amount is much smaller, with the Angolan Ministry of Finance claiming that CIF have made available to the GRN 'only' $2.9 billion. These funds were supposedly earmarked to carry out various construction projects, such as the building of a new international airport in Luanda, roads and railway rehabilitation, as well as drainage in Luanda city. The message disseminated by the Angolan state is that due to difficulties in securing financing, the Angolan government instructed the Angolan Ministry of Finance to secure domestic funding through the sale of treasury bonds to the value of $3.5 billion (Angolan Ministry of Finance 2007).

Yet CIF, increasingly known for its opacity, has generated considerable international controversy following the announcement of controversial loan agreements in Latin America (Levkowitz *et al.* 2009) and Guinea. In this context, Vines *et al.* (2009, 51) has pointed to the importance of the CIF directors' personal connections both with Chinese and Angolan officials in securing prominent contracts in Angola.

The third channel of funding will come from the China Development Bank (CDB), which has shown interest in investing in Angola's agriculture potential. A reported $1 billion has been earmarked for investment in this sector, and the CDB's head, Chen Yuan, has stated that this amount may be extended if necessary (Agence France-Presse 2009a). Further to this, the Industrial and Commercial Bank of Bank of China (ICBC)[10] has also made a trip to Angola with the possible intention of investing in Angola (Angop 2009). Previously a fully-fledged policy bank, CDB is in the process of commercialising, although this may have been shelved indefinitely due to the 2008 financial crisis. ICBC, however, is China's largest commercial bank. That both entities are interested in Angolan projects is interesting, as it may serve to broaden a relationship that is still largely based on trading oil.

Despite these additional financing structures, it is the role of the China Exim Bank that has arguably received the most scrutiny, particularly due to claims that the China Exim Bank is heedless of risk, and is a mechanism to facilitate Chinese access to Angolan oil and political favour. These claims will be examined below.

Negotiating risk

China Exim Bank is the sole agency for the provision of Chinese government concessional loans, distinguished from commercial loans by their lower-than-market interest rates, a long grace period – or both, as in the case of China Exim Bank's loan to Angola. The World Bank, which has a Memorandum of Understanding (MOU) with the China Exim Bank regarding financing infrastructure in developing countries, does not have a unified position on how to quantify Exim Bank loans. According to a recent report by the World Bank, these loans are 'marginally concessional, although significantly less so than those associated with ODA [official development assistance]' (Foster *et al.* 2008, vi). However, the same report attributes a 50.3% grant element to at least the first $2 billion tranche of China Exim Bank financing (*ibid.*, 46), whereas to qualify for ODA, it need only be 25%.

Despite assertions by Martyn Davies that Chinese companies and policy banks have a 'risk model that is different' (Davies 2008, 151), somehow implying that they are less bound to short-term profit than their Western counterparts, the China Exim Bank in fact has been exceedingly cautious in its dealings with the Angolan government and remains wary of African projects, due to the perceived high level of risk involved.[11]

Exim Bank's lending policy is to structure a loan so that there is a revenue stream that will be able to support the debt repayment.[12] Consequently, the recipient country can use exports of natural resources to China to repay the loan, as in the case of Angola, or part of the infrastructure financing will be used to develop natural resource extraction for collateral, as in the case of the Democratic Republic of Congo (DRC).[13] Furthermore, the mechanism whereby the contracted construction companies are paid directly by the China Exim Bank ensures that China Exim has full control of project disbursements, in an attempt to mitigate the perceived risk of the loan money entering the Angolan financial system (and then no doubt disappearing). In addition to this, during the negotiations, Exim Bank initially demanded 1% interest on top of the agreement's interest rate payments as insurance, rejecting the Angolan Finance Ministry's offer of a sovereign guarantee. It was only allegedly when the Chinese Ministry of Foreign Affairs intervened to persuade Exim Bank to waive this insurance payment that the loan structure was agreed upon.[14] According to an Angolan observer, China Exim Bank was also initially 'very inflexible' in terms of the projects that it was negotiating to finance.[15]

The World Bank has locked horns with China Exim Bank arguing that given the Exim Bank requirement for a guaranteed revenue stream, the loan should be commercial, and thus not require a sovereign guarantee. Such matters came to a head during the negotiations over a proposed $9 billion resources-for-infrastructure deal by a consortium of Chinese companies led by China Exim Bank in the DRC.[16] The IMF and World Bank managed to persuade Exim Bank to drop the requirement of a sovereign guarantee (Reuters 2009). In the case of Angola, as discussed above, Exim Bank had initially not even accepted a sovereign guarantee (preferring a commercially structured 1% interest payment built into the loan's interest) until political pressure from the Chinese Ministry of Finance was brought to bear. This is hardly an exhibition of a 'risk model that is different'.

Interestingly, the Chinese Ministry of Finance appears to agree with the World Bank's position. This is evident not only through the outcome of the negotiations surrounding the Angolan interest rate, but also due to the perspective of the Ministry that the Exim Bank, as a policy bank, should pursue foreign policy objectives, and not make a profit.[17] It was even commented that the Exim Bank should commercialise in order to remove the question marks about its agenda and motives. For the time being it appears that Exim Bank *does* follow a political agenda. Nevertheless, it must be pointed out that this is under duress. The Bank, it appears, would prefer to structure more commercially-oriented deals. That this does not occur provides an insight into the competing agendas at the policy-making level in China, and may therefore fluctuate according to the balance of power in Beijing as the various ministries, policy banks and state-owned enterprises compete for influence in the State Council.

Financing access to oil

The implication of previous reports on China's infrastructure financing is that its provision also secures Chinese companies access to exploitable resources (Foster *et al.* 2008). This certainly appeared to be initially the case in Angola. Chinese interests first entered this sector in 2004 when China Petroleum and Chemical Corporation, (Sinopec) bought a 50% stake of Block 18 for the reported sum of $725 million (Financial Express 2006), coinciding with the disbursement of the first tranche of China Exim Bank's financing. Sinopec's entry into Angola's oil blocks was originally marred by controversy, as it appeared that Shell, the former owner of the 50% stake, had several months previously signed a purchase agreement with Indian oil company ONGC Videsh. This deal was, however, refused approval by the national state-owned oil company Sonangol, also the industry's concessionaire, as Sonangol had not apparently been previously consulted. The stake was then instead awarded to Sinopec (Vines *et al.* 2009, 17). In late 2004–2005, Sinopec then acquired Block 3/80, owned previously by Total, after Sonangol did not renew the French company's contract.[18] Interestingly, Sinopec's entry into Angola coincided with the announcement of China Exim Bank's $2 billion loan facility to the Angolan government to finance infrastructure reconstruction.

Particularly as this was the first entry of a Chinese national oil company into what was considered a strategic African country, China Exim Bank is believed to have indirectly supported Sinopec's oil acquisition through the provision of the loan facility (Downs 2007, 53). Furthermore, as observed by Lee and Shalmon (2008, 120) although there is no explicit link to China Exim Bank's loan to Angola and the awarding of oil blocks to Sinopec, 'there is a strong suggestion that they are linked. The coincidence is too great'. However, although China Exim Bank's loans to Angola are speculated to have assisted Sinopec's bids for Angolan oil blocks, this has not in fact continued to be the case. Indeed, Chinese national oil companies are very junior partners in the Angolan oil industry.

It initially appeared that Sinopec had made rapid inroads into Angola's oil industry. After forming a joint venture Sinopec-Sonangol International (SSI) with company Sonangol, Sinopec (the 75% shareholder in the joint-venture) acquired equity in several other Angola oil blocks, attaining 27.5%, 40% and 20% in the offshore blocks 17, 18 and 15 respectively. The signature bonuses of $1.1 billion for the concessions in block 17 and 18 were the highest ever offered in the history of Angola's oil industry (Burke *et al.* 2007, 37). Sinopec had also been in negotiations with the Angolan government to develop a 200,000 barrels-per-day oil refinery at Lobito.

Despite such a promising start Sinopec has, however, now largely retreated. The refinery deal was called off in March 2007, reportedly due to a lack of consensus as to the intended destination of the refined product, although it is unclear which side imposed the deal-breaker. It emerged in late 2008 that American engineering firm, Kellogg Brown and Root (KBR), had been awarded the contract for construction on the refinery, then estimated to have a cost of $8 billion. Almost immediately after announcing an end to negotiations regarding the refinery in Lobito, Sinopec then also withdrew from its stakes in blocks 15, 17 and 18. Amid much controversy as to who would assume Sinopec's shares, it appears that China Sonangol International Holding had, as well as taking on the exploring rights to block 3/80, assumed control of the blocks before a more permanent equity partner had been secured (Campos and Vines 2007, 16).[19] Then in October 2008, Sinopec and CNOOC negotiated with Marathon the purchase of a 20% stake in Bloc 32 for $1.8 billion (Winning and Faucon 2008). But in October 2009, Sonangol – as existing equity holder – exercised its right of first refusal and blocked the Chinese purchase by announcing its own intention to buy it.

Despite speculations of a link between China Exim Bank's inaugural loan and Sinopec's first successful bid for equity in block 18, there is in fact little evidence to support continued preferential treatment at the bidding table for Chinese oil companies due to extensive Chinese loans. Indeed, Chinese companies do not possess the technology to exploit Angola's deep and ultra-deep blocks in the Gulf of Guinea and so have been side-lined since 2006 (Downs 2007, 46–7).

Any aspirations the Chinese Government may have had of smoothing the entry of national oil companies into Angola have thus been thwarted for practical reasons. Exim Bank has so far had far more success in facilitating the entry of Chinese construction companies into the Angolan market rather than in lubricating some Chinese ostensible 'takeover' of Angola's oil industry.

Angola's bid to diversify finance partners

Particularly in the last few years and on the back of a strong oil price and Angola's debt normalisation, Luanda has approved an increasing number of credit lines from a number of countries. Aside from the material assistance that China's Exim Bank loans have provided, the provision of funds seems to have acted as a kind of financial catalyst for other flows of financing from other sources.[20] For instance, in 2007 Spain alone provided $600 million in construction aid (Angop 2007). Furthermore Canada's Export Development Bank has signed an agreement with Angola's Banco de Poupança e Crédito for $1 billion to finance government infrastructure projects and $16 million for private enterprise projects. Brazil's Banco Nacional de Desenvolvimento Económico e Social (BNDES) has already disbursed $1.5 billion to fund the purchase of Brazilian construction equipment in Angola in the first five months of the 2009 and has also offered $250 million to fund projects in Angola. Angola has recently attracted the interest of other financiers, most notably the World Bank, which will extend loans of $1 billion from 2009 to 2013 to assist with economic diversification.

Such developments point to a considerable thawing of relations between Angola and international financial institutions. In 2004, negotiations with the IMF had collapsed over the loans' conditionalities, leading Angola to turn to China for financing. It appears that the World Bank then pursued a different approach in order to avoid marginalisation by other emerging financiers, choosing to pursue co-operation with China Exim Bank in Africa. The Bank has also been mollified by the Angolan Government's policy of debt normalisation in an attempt to move away from using oil as collateral for commercial loans. An agreement is in place for Angola to service its Paris Club debt. The bulk of the $2.3 billion had been paid by December 2007, but more than $800 million in interest was still owed. Plans are in place to have the debt repaid. It is hoped that debt regularisation will then further allow the government to access credit from a more diversified bouquet of country lenders, rather than leaning solely on China.

Credit lines with the goal of export promotion from European countries, while forthcoming, are not comparable in size to those of China. In the first half of 2009 Germany extended $1.7 billion to Angola and Portugal offered $500 million. The US Exim Bank has offered $120 million and Britain $70 million in credit in comparison. These credit extensions may have been instituted as other institutions became emboldened by the confidence their Chinese counterparts were showing in Angola. It is more likely, however, that these government fear that their own companies are losing out to Chinese companies that, it is perceived, are given an unfair advantage through state support. Their fears are largely unwarranted however. China is *not* the only country to extend credit lines to the Angolan government. Brazil and Portugal have for years extended oil-backed credit lines to facilitate the import of their companies' products and services, particularly in the construction sector (Burke and Corkin 2006, 16). These are primarily geared towards facilitating infrastructure construction, a stated priority of the Angolan Government. Consequently, barring the size of the loans, there is little difference between the Chinese credit lines and those of other countries. *All* the credit lines are contingent on their use to purchase products and services from their own companies respectively.

Thus far from allowing China preferential treatment as a trading or investment partner, Chinese financing seems to have encouraged other countries to extend credit lines in order to also allow their own companies and products to compete on a similar footing. This has been strongly promoted by Luanda. Angola is arguably one of the sub-Saharan African countries most jealous of its sovereignty and the Angolan executive is careful not to let any singular foreign trade partner dominate the domestic political or economic arena. Angola, despite international concerns – particularly in the context of strengthening China–Angola relations – will strongly resist becoming or being perceived as a client state of any other country.

Evaluating the 'strategic partnership'

Given that Angola has been China's top African trading partner since 2007, there is a marked disparity in the level of China–Angola trade and the corresponding level of China–Angola investment, relative to other resource-rich African countries. With $78.48 million, Angola ranked twelfth in terms of its Chinese foreign direct investment (FDI) stock in 2007, albeit that Chinese FDI stock in the top 11 African countries exceeded $100 billion. In 2006, Chinese FDI accounted for 0.3% of Angola's total FDI stock and 0.64% in 2007 (UNCTAD 2008). This seems to infer that while Angola is considered an important source of oil, particularly within the West African region, Chinese companies do not regard Angola as a major strategic location for investment, beyond acquisitions in the oil industry. This *may* change given the recent interest of additional Chinese banks such as ICBC and CDB, however, as it stands; according to Vines *et al.* (2009, 47) the Angolans themselves suggest that Chinese interests in the DRC will eclipse those in Angola. Furthermore, various Chinese think-tanks have voiced the opinion that South Africa is in fact considered to be a more strategic African partner for Beijing.[21]

This may be explained by several factors. Firstly, Angola's investment climate is severely problematic. Angola is ranked by the World Bank's 2009 *Doing business* report as 168 out of 181 and according to this report, although ranked 53rd for 'protecting investors', Angola has a ranking of 156 for starting a business and 179 for 'enforcing a contract'. There is little wonder therefore that most Chinese construction companies' entry into Angola's market has been through a tightly managed high-level bilateral agreement between the Angolan government and China Exim Bank or CIF. A consequence of this is that the involvement of Chinese construction companies cannot be considered direct investment, given the mechanism of the loan, as described above. Furthermore, Angola, due to its relative lack of infrastructure and integration into the wider region – a legacy of decades of civil war – is not a strategic location for export-oriented manufacturing, nor is it a particularly attractive market, with a population of approximately only 16 million, almost 80% of which are considered to be impoverished. Its highly Eurocentric elite look towards Paris and Lisbon (and to a lesser extent, Brazil) for consumption. In contrast, resource-rich countries such as Sudan or the DRC, which share a similar profile to Angola, boast much higher Chinese FDI stocks. The significant difference between these countries and Angola is that the political elite have retained majority ownership of their resources.

Where Chinese companies *are* interested in investing is in the oil sector. The Angolan government, which for decades has directed the Angolan oil industry through its parastatal company Sonangol, has been less open to Chinese investment in the oil industry than originally expected. As noted above, several blocks that various Chinese national oil companies had shown a keen interest in purchasing were denied them. This may well be for pragmatic reasons; Chinese companies have yet to develop the technology required to exploit deep and ultra-deep water oil resources. Indeed, they have been looking to learn such techniques in partnership with Western oil majors in Angola. Nevertheless, it sends a strong political message to Beijing and points to the shrewd management of the oil industry on the part of the Angolan government, whose management of increasing Chinese interest in the oil sector has been much more skilful than Nigeria's (Vines *et al.* 2009).

Angola for its part has leveraged its growing relationship with China on several levels: the international, the national and the regional. In the past few years Luanda has acquired access to various lines of credit from a variety of different partners, as discussed above. This points to the Angolan government's successful strategy of diversification, compared to the situation of a few years' previously. As noted, the Angolan government has always been fiercely protective of its sovereignty, eschewing an IMF structural adjustment package in 2004 for China's less conditional financing. Considered a 'quick-fix' at the time, Luanda is now wary of allowing Chinese interests to hold too much sway in the economy. Nevertheless, Chinese financing has been important. It is viewed in some quarters as having acted as a kind of catalyst to attracting financing from other countries.[22] Previously, other avenues to secure financing were limited as Angola only received a sovereign credit rating (B+) in May 2010 (Theunissen 2010) and attempts to sell bonds on the international market had not as yet proven very successful.

Similarly, on the domestic front, in the early years following the end of the civil war, China Exim Bank's loans provided the means to begin the national reconstruction project. Aside from its practical necessity following the destruction caused by the civil war, the MPLA government required Chinese financial assistance to kick-start recovery as a state-building device through infrastructure creation in the expansion of state capacity. This was essential from the perspective of political survival and proved successful, given the MPLA's landslide victory in the legislative elections of 2008.

Conclusions

Angola's relationship with China seems to be maturing from a heady embrace of mutual convenience to a reassessment of each other's strategic significance as partners. From the perspective of Beijing, the question has been raised as to whether such relations are sustainable as they currently stand.[23] Far from serving as a kind of 'model' for other resource rich countries' relations with China, it has been suggested that the strategic partnership forged between Luanda and Beijing was done so at an opportune moment of equal need, for financing and oil resources respectively.[24]

Furthermore, the Chinese Ministry of Foreign Affairs, in view of Beijing's previously problematic involvement in Angola's history, may have felt that it was politically expedient to conclude a deal, overruling any reservations that Exim Bank may have harboured.[25] The outcome of the arrangement, has – contrary to the expectations of some – *not* rendered Chinese oil companies greater access to Angola oil blocks, although supply of oil as collateral has been secured.

For Angola, China remains an important trading partner, whose demand for Angolan crude oil and willingness to provide credit lines have taken on increasing significance following the oil price fluctuations in the wake of the financial crisis. Angola, as a key oil supplier to China, is of similar consequence as a trading partner. Yet Angola balances the need to retain China Exim Bank as a financing partner with denying the less experienced Chinese national oil companies access to exploration blocks that they cannot operate. Should they have been predicated on acquiring oil at source through equity provided by the China Exim Bank, other Chinese policy-making bodies involved may be reassessing the their motives for entering Angola.

Consequently, because the Sino-Angolan relationship hinges largely on oil, despite its importance, this does not bode well for its sustainability. Political posturing and empirical evidence indicates that both China and Angola see each other as necessary strategic allies for the foreseeable future, but this may obscure what is in fact an uneasy marriage of convenience.

Notes

1. Interview, Beijing, 29 October 2009.
2. Interview, Beijing, 28 October 2009.
3. Angolan Minister of Finance, Carlos Albert Lopes, broadcast on Radio Nacional de Angola, 4pm, 9 July 2010.
4. The interest rate is quoted according to the Angolan Ministry of Finance. Libor, according to the British Banker's Association, is the most widely used benchmark or reference rate for short term interest rates.
5. Interview, Luanda, 30 May 2007.
6. The MPLA is reported to have taken credit for large-scale infrastructure projects undertaken by the Angolan government in the run-up to the national elections in late 2008.
7. Interview, Beijing, 28 October 2009.

8. The Chinese government has distanced itself from CIF, but it is likely CIF has some Chinese government connections (Vines *et al.* 2009, 51; Levkowitz *et al.* 2009, 33). China Development Bank, while currently a state-owned policy bank, is marked to be fully commercialised. This process was, however, halted due to the financial crisis beginning 2008.
9. Interview with a director of a foreign-invested bank, Luanda, 7 June 2006.
10. ICBC is China's largest commercial bank and currently the largest bank in the world by asset value. ICBC also has a strategic partnership with Standard Bank, Africa's largest Bank. Standard Bank has had a representative office in Angola for some years but does not yet have a commercial banking license.
11. Personal correspondence, Beijing, 27 October 2009.
12. Interview, Beijing, 14 October 2009.
13. Ecuador was originally required by China Exim Bank to put up the assets of its Central Bank for collateral as the country had no cash crop or natural resource exports to back the loan (Agence France-Presse 2009b).
14. Interview, Beijing, 29 October 2009.
15. Interview, Beijing, 28 October 2009.
16. The deal is widely believed to have been modelled on the co-operation agreement signed with Angola. The IMF eventually succeeded in persuading China Exim Bank to retract its requirement of a sovereign guarantee, but the deal was reduced to US$6 billion for rehabilitating the mining industry and the plans for US$3 billion in 'social infrastructure projects' were scrapped.
17. Interview, Beijing, 29 October 2009.
18. It was later agreed between Sonangol and Sinopec that China Sonangol International Holding (CSIH), jointly owned by Sonangol and Beiya International Development Ltd., would explore this block. China Sonangol International Holding (CSIH), a subsidiary of Sonangol and Beiya International Development Ltd. that invests in industrial, petroleum and infrastructure investment not only in Angola but also in other countries including Argentina and Venezuela, now has equity in several Angolan blocks, having temporarily assumed management of some of the blocks initially purchased by Sinopec.
19. CSIH now has equity in several Angolan blocks, having temporarily assumed management of some of the blocks initially purchased by Sinopec (Campos and Vines 2007, 16).
20. Interview, Beijing, 28 October 2008.
21. Interviews Shanghai, 17 September 2009; Beijing, 16 October 2009.
22. Interview, Beijing, 28 October 2009.
23. Interview, Beijing, 16 October 2009.
24. Interview, Beijing, 9 September 2009.
25. Interview, Beijing, 29 October 2009.

Notes on contributor

Lucy Corkin is a Research Associate of the Africa–Asia Centre at the School of Oriental and African Studies, University of London. Between 2006 and 2008, as Projects Director of the Centre for Chinese Studies, Stellenbosch University, South Africa, Lucy co-ordinated and led research projects funded by DFID and the Rockefeller Foundation investigating China's relations with various African countries.

References

Angolan Ministry of Finance. 2007. Ministry of Finance denies misuse of Chinese loans. Angolan Ministry of Finance Press Release, October 17.
Angop. 2007. Country and Spain sign investment protection accord. *Angop*, November 21.
Angop. 2009. President Dos Santos receives China commercial bank official. *Angop*, October 16.
Agence France-Presse. 2009a. Angola wins new billion dollar loan from China. *Agence France-Presse*, March 12.

Agence France-Presse. 2009b. Ecuador leader: Negotiating with China like pulling teeth. *Agence France-Presse*, December 5.

Burke, C., and L. Corkin. 2006. *China's interest and activity in Africa's construction and infrastructure sectors*. Report prepared for the Department of International Development (DFID). China, Stellenbosch: Centre for Chinese Studies, Stellenbosch University.

Burke, C., L. Corkin, and N. Tay. 2007. *China's engagement of Africa: Preliminary scoping of African Case studies: A scoping exercise evaluating China's engagement of six African case studies*. Prepared for the Rockefeller Foundation, Stellenbosch: Centre for Chinese Studies, Stellenbosch University.

Campos, I., and A. Vines. 2007. Angola and China: A pragmatic partnership. Paper presented at the CSIS conference, 'Prospects for Improving US–China–Africa Cooperation', December 5, Washington.

Chen, C., P. Chiu, R. Orr, and A. Goldstein. 2007. An empirical analysis of Chinese construction firms' entry into Africa. Paper presented at international symposium on Advancement of Construction Management and Real Estate, Sydney, Australia.

Corkin, L. 2007a. 'Angola Model' sets the trend for Chinese funding. *African Energy* 120: 6–8.

Corkin, L. 2007b. China's contribution to the development of African infrastructure through investment in the extractive industries. *AFRODAD Occasional Paper* 8.

Corkin, L. 2008a. China's interest in Angola's infrastructure and construction sectors. In *China's New Role in Africa and the South*, ed. D. Guerrero and F. Manji, 134–50. Oxford: Fahamu.

Corkin, L. 2008b. Oil's fair in loans and war: An overview of China–Angola relations. In *Crouching Tiger, Hidden Dragon?: Africa and China*, ed. K. Ampiah and S. Naidu, 25–34. Scottsville: University of KwaZulu-Natal Press.

Corkin, L. 2008c. AERC scoping exercise on China–Africa relations: The case of Angola. *African Economic Research Consortium*, January.

Davies, M. 2008. Special economic zones: China's developmental model comes to Africa. In *China into Africa: Trade, Aid and Influence*, ed. R. Rotberg, 136–45. Washington DC: Brookings Institution Press.

Desphande, G., and H. Gupta. 1986. *United front against imperialism: China's foreign policy in Africa*. Mumbai: Somiya Publications.

Downs, E. 2007. The fact and fiction of Sino-Africa energy relations. *China Security* 3, no. 3: 42–68.

Financial Express. 2006. China beats ONGC, gets Angola block. *Financial Express*, July 15. http://www.financialexpress.com/news/Sinopec-beats-ONGC,-gets-Angola-block-/171139/ (accessed March 15, 2011).

Foster, V., W. Zutterfield, C. Chen, and N. Pushak. 2008. *China's emerging role in Africa*. Washington DC: World Bank.

Lee, H., and D. Shalmon. 2008. Searching for oil: China's oil strategies in Africa. In *China into Africa: Trade, aid and influence*, ed. Robert I. Rotberg, 109–36. Washington, DC: Brookings Institution Press.

Levkowitz, L., R. McLellan, and J. Warner. 2009. *The 88 Queensway Group: A case study in Chinese investors in Angola and beyond*. Washington DC: US–China Economic and Security Review Commission.

Reuters. 2009. *Mining guarantees withdrawn from China's DRC investment deal under IMF pressure*, 19 August. http://www.mineweb.com/mineweb/view/mineweb/en/page72068?oid = 87733&sn = Detail (accessed November 10, 2009).

Snow, P. 1988. *The star raft*. London: Weidenfeld and Nicolson.

Stratfor. 2009. China: A new approach on African oil? *Stratfor*, November 6.

Taylor, I. 2006. *China and Africa: Engagement and compromise*. London: Routledge.

Taylor, I. 2009. *China's new role in Africa*. Boulder, CO: Lynne Rienner.

Theunissen, G. 2010. Angola gets ratings: Paves way for sale of bonds. *Bloomberg*, May 19.

UNCTAD. 2008. *World Investment Directory, Volume X: Africa*. New York: UNCTAD.

Vines, A., L. Wong, M. Weimer, and I. Campos. 2009. *Thirst for African oil: Asian national oil companies in Nigeria and Angola*. London: Chatham House, August.

Winning, D., and B. Faucon. 2008. Sinopec, CNOOC to agree on $1.8B for Angola Asset. *Dow Jones Newswires* http://www.rigzone.com/news/article.asp?a_id=67348 (July 10, 2009).

Sino-Zambian relations: 'An all-weather friendship' weathering the storm

Dominik Kopiński and Andrzej Polus

University of Wrocław, Poland

> Sino-Zambian relations are exceptional to a remarkable degree, and do not seem to fall into the common pattern used to describe the Sino-African relationship as part of a so-called 'new scramble for Africa'. Zambia is a country where both positive and negative developments took place earlier than elsewhere on the African continent and, in this respect, Zambia has always been one step ahead of the rest of its peers. This study is divided into three parts. The first part presents a historical overview of diplomatic relations between China and Zambia. The second part deals with the domestic politics of Zambia and the usage by Zambian elites of the Chinese presence as an argument in internal political discourses. The third part focuses on emerging patterns of Chinese investment in Zambia, and tries to unpack some of the common myths pertaining to the scope and nature of China's engagement in Africa, based on the Zambian example.

According to common understandings of China–Africa relations, the African continent, with its significant supply of raw materials and relatively weak socio-political structures, is a place where neo-mercantilist China is tapping into the crude materials necessary to sustain its booming economy (Shinn 2009). This situation is often pictured as a new 'scramble for Africa', where both state-owned and private corporations are seeking to subordinate the continent and where options for African states are being delimited to either Beijing's or Washington's 'consensus'. This conventional description is normative, and it fairly structures the general perception of Sino-African relations. We, however, want to challenge this narrative by investigating the case of Zambia. We believe that Sino-Zambian relations are exceptional to a remarkable degree, and do not seem to fall into the pattern used to describe Sino-African relationships elsewhere.

We embark on this quest with an assertion that Zambia is a country where both positive and negative developments have taken place earlier than elsewhere in the African continent. In other words, during the postcolonial era Zambia was always one step ahead of the rest of sub-Saharan Africa. As Alyster Fraser points out, 'independence, one-party rule, economic collapse, adjustment, and democratisation all came earlier in Zambia than in neighbouring countries' (Fraser 2009, 302). We believe that this view can be equally accurate in describing contemporary Sino-Zambian relations, for they offer a great deal of novelty, indeed, a uniqueness vis-à-vis other African states. Consequently, the Zambian case, *toutes proportions gardee*, might be instructive for other African states.

We support our view with the following arguments. Among all African states hosting Chinese investments, in Zambia anti-Chinese sentiments absolutely hit the roof. They leaked into and were prompted by internal politics, as anti-Chinese rhetoric was thoroughly exploited by Michael Sata during his 2006 presidential campaign, a case arguably without precedence in Africa. The campaign severely strained Sino-Zambian relations, which had encountered difficulties, particularly in the Copperbelt region where 'the Chinese' were held accountable for tragic accidents involving a number of Zambian workers. Moreover, this was the very first time China openly violated its 'non-interference rule', when the Chinese Ambassador to Zambia, Li Baodong, threatened: 'We shall have nothing to do with Zambia if Sata wins the elections and goes ahead to recognise Taiwan' (Agence France-Press [AFP], 5 September 2006). The long-hailed 'all-weather friendship' between the two countries was put to the test.

Yet today, amid controversies, especially in the Copperbelt and Lusaka regions where the Chinese presence is the most visible, Sino-Zambian relations seem to be thriving. When President Hu Jintao visited Zambia on 3 February 2007, 'his stay in Zambia was considerably longer than in any of the other seven African states. This was interpreted by many observers as a clear indication of the importance China attributed to its relations with Zambia' (Davies 2008, 45). There is no doubt that China is regarded by the Zambian government as a top priority investor of today, and possibly the key strategic investor of tomorrow – it was in Zambia that China's leader announced plans to set up the very first Multi-facility Special Economic Zone in Africa.

In order to better understand the case of Zambia, both as a forerunner of socio-political developments in sub-Saharan Africa and a strategic partner of China on the continent, it is necessary to take into account the following, distinctive characteristics of Zambia. Zambia has never experienced a successful military coup. Moreover, despite enormous internal ethnic and lingual heterogeneity, Zambia remains remarkably stable – the 'tribalism' usually associated with African politics is not as intense in Zambia as in other sub-Saharan states. Another feature is the existence of relatively strong civil organisations when compared with other African states (in the mid-1990s there were over 9,000 registered non-government organisations (NGOs) in this country). Trade unions especially have a long tradition of public protest; it is worth mentioning that the Zambia Confederation of Trade Unions acted as the opposition to the United National Independence Party (UNIP) government (Burnell 2001, 139–40; Momba 2003, 45). Indeed, miners were strategically placed not only in the Zambian economy, but also in Zambia's politics; the trade unions were the only real internal force able to challenge the one-party state. Similarly, in 2001 a coalition of NGOs and opposition parties resisted President Frederick Chiluba's bid for a third term in office (Tripp 2009, 148).

The role of copper

Zambia became independent in 1964, and because of rich copper deposits was perceived as potentially the most prosperous newly independent state in sub-Saharan Africa (Larmer 2007, 191). After over 50 years of independence however, Zambia is now one of the world's poorest states, and despite its vast mineral possessions, two-thirds of Zambia's citizens live below the poverty line. The country is often used as a prime example of the 'natural resource course' hypothesis and its postcolonial history can be summarised as the 'typical' manifestation of underdevelopment with a monoculture economy fully dependent on the world prices of primary commodities.

Yet after gaining independence from Britain, there was a lot of hope for Zambia's future. In Kaunda's words, Zambia was 'born with a copper spoon in its mouth'. The country was the world's third largest copper producer, and the British GDP per capita was just seven times higher than the Zambian (today this ratio is 28:1). From the outset, however, the country's dependence on 'red metal' has been at the very heart of its economic problems, and gaining control over copper deposits has played an important role in internal politics (Shaw 1976). In 1969 most mining companies were nationalised by Kenneth Kaunda, who pursued a 'socialist' path officially known as African Humanism (Kaunda 1967). Soon afterwards, problems began to amass. A peak copper output of 750,000 tones in 1973 was followed by an oil crisis, and copper prices drastically declined. In 1982 the government set up the Zambian Consolidated Copper Mines (ZCCM) and acquired the majority share in the company. Prosperity did not follow, however, and in the 1990s the Zambian copper industry was already 'dead on its feet' (Taylor 2006, 179) due to a combination of mismanagement and external factors. Subsequently, under privatisation schemes, ZCCM was unbundled and between 1992 and 2000 sold off to investors from Canada, Britain, India, Switzerland, South Africa and China (Craig 2001). The injection of fresh capital of about $1 billion (Ruffini 2006, 39) helped to reverse the prolonged downturn trend in copper production in Zambia.

Besides being a symbol of national pride and an important factor in the process of national consolidation after independence, the copper industry has played a vital role in domestic politics.[1] Before privatisation it was a source of revenues that were used by the government to stabilise the neo-patrimonial political regime. Martin Meredith estimates that in 1980 Kenneth Kaunda controlled 40,000 patronage positions in Lusaka alone (Meredith 2006, 380). If we look at Zambia from the perspective of the relative stability of patron-client relations in Zambian politics, which have guaranteed a foreseeable political process, then we will see that state control of copper revenues was a necessary factor to maintain political permanence. From this standpoint, Structural Adjustment Programmes, and successful external pressure on the post-1991 Zambian governments aimed at copper industry privatisation, has created a situation in which the old political habits and governance structures still exist, but the government is unable to maintain them, which in turn produces instability. Foreign ownership of the mines reduces resources available for local elites for political bargaining.

Sino-Zambian relations

Ian Taylor has noted that the importance of China's relations with Zambia can be explained by 'a consideration of two factors: Zambia's geo-strategic position, and the personality of Kenneth Kaunda and his political orientation' (Taylor 2006, 165). The postcolonial history of Zambia is associated with Kenneth Kaunda. Kaunda was a champion of the African liberation movements as well as a strong supporter of the Non-Alignment Movement (NAM). China was an important actor during the conference in Bandung, where NAM was created and the organisation can be seen as arguably the first visible network in Sino-African relations. During his time in power, Kaunda visited China four times, and it is worth mentioning that Mao Zedong articulated his idea of the Three Worlds in 1974 during a conversation with the Zambian president (Lanteigne 2009, 132). It was also Kenneth Kaunda who coined the term 'all-weather friendship' to define relations between the People's Republic of China and the newly independent African states.[2] This partnership was crucial for Zambia for both pragmatic and ideological reasons. Regardless of the internal turbulence in the 1960s and 1970s, China was an alternative source for various sorts of aid for Zambia while it was heavily involved in its anti-apartheid campaign, and a counterbalance to relations with the Soviet Union and the Western Bloc.

By and large, China's relations with Africa in the 1960s and 1970s concentrated on Beijing's support for liberation movements, while the newly independent African states provided support to China in the international arena (Mwanawina 2008, 1), mainly in terms of China's bid for a permanent place on the United Nations (UN) Security Council. The most visible symbol of Sino-African relations during the Cold War was the Tanzania–Zambia (called TAZARA or Tam–Zam) railway (Sautman and Yan Hairong 2008, 91) built by the Chinese in order to bypass Rhodesia after Ian Smith's unilateral declaration of independence. The TAZARA project, finished in 1975, was not only the third biggest infrastructure project in Africa but because it provided a transport link between the Copperbelt and Dar es Salaam it was a visible sign of joint Sino-African co-operation at the peak of the Rhodesia crisis.

After Kaunda's loss of office in 1990, Sino-Zambian relations did not worsen, but because of the political transformation taking place in South Africa and structural changes in the international milieu, the Cold War rhetoric of anti-apartheid and anti-imperialism was no longer relevant as a basis for co-operation. However, African governments support Beijing's vision of the 'multi-polar world order' and both sides have criticised agriculture subsidies in the EU and USA. This idea was clearly expressed by Kaunda's successor as President, Frederick Chiluba speaking at the China–Africa Co-operation Forum (FOCAC) opening ceremony in 2000, when he stated:

> [Developed countries] are not prepared to discuss the issues of justice and fair play concerning the international trade and commercial sector, which imposes considerable suffering and privation on developing countries ... [T]he developing world continues to subsidise consumption of the developed world, through an iniquitous trade system. The existing structure is designed to consign us to perpetual poverty and underdevelopment [...] It is unrealistic to expect support, relief or respite from those who benefit from the status quo (Hairong and Sautman 2009).

Additionally, China's lack of a colonial legacy strengthened Beijing's position in Africa and the vast majority of African states pursued the one-China policy (Negi 2008, 42; Taylor, 2009). The additional advantage for China comes from the numerical support of the African nations in the UN General Assembly. Despite backing China's claims to a permanent seat in the UN Security Council in the 1960s, the current African support seems to be vital with regard to Western rhetoric on human rights violations and Beijing's policy towards Tibet. However, the most important aspect of Sino-Zambian relations during the post-Kaunda era have been Chinese investments in the mining industry (China is now the third biggest foreign investor in Zambia). On the official level of government-to-government interactions, China has stressed its Third World credentials, and Kenneth Kaunda's expression of an 'all-weather friendship' is still used as the mantra of official meetings.

Chinese investments in Zambia

Chinese companies are pushing ahead with a massive investment drive in Africa. In Zambia, China has recently become the third largest investor after South Africa and the UK. According to the Zambian Development Agency (ZDA), Chinese investment in Zambia has exceeded $1 billion and created about 15,000 job opportunities (ZDA *Chinese Investments in Zambia* 3 February 2010). The actual investment footprint is more difficult to gauge. Data comprising Chinese FDI in Zambia is not readily available, and ZDA publishes only 'investment pledges' that can diverge from the real FDI accumulation. Nevertheless, there are two general patterns to be discerned. First, in terms of volume, Chinese investments in Zambia mainly pour into extractive industries. Between 2000 and 2009, investment in mining constituted as much as 89% of all Chinese FDI pledges ($5.5 billion). Chinese companies are pursuing a strategy targeted at tapping into Zambia's rich mineral deposits, mainly copper, but also zinc and nickel. Due to recent oil and gas discoveries, Zambia's attractiveness will probably increase even further. Chinese investors, namely the Zhonghui Guohua Industry Limited Group and the State Grid Corporation of China, have already demonstrated interest in exploiting the newly discovered deposits of hydrocarbons located in the Mwinilunga district in the North-Western province (*Lusaka Times*, 17 March 2009). Secondly, the composition of Chinese FDI with regard to its source is dominated by large, state-led, policy-driven, publicly owned companies, although small-scale investment has been gaining more importance.

Most recently the demand for copper, a key component of electrical wiring and cables, has risen due to China's economic growth. In 2009, China's economy consumed 30% of the world's production of copper. It is predicted that by 2030 it will account for 50% of the demand for copper. The growing demand has helped the Zambian copper production surge in recent years. In 2010 output is projected to increase by 5% to 700,000 tonnes[3] from 662,000 tonnes in 2009 and 575,000 tonnes in 2008. This rise in production is expected to be mainly caused by an increase in production at Lumwana and the resumption of production at the Luanshya Copper Mines. According to ZDA, only about 5% of Zambia's copper is extracted by Chinese firms. However, almost the entire copper output is sold overseas, on the London Metal Exchange, where China is one of the largest buyers of Zambian copper (estimated at 20% of the annual copper production of Zambia). The largest Chinese players to be found in the Zambian mining sector include the Zhougui Mining Group (the largest private investor in Zambian history after having signed the Investment Promotion and Protection Agreement (IPPA) with the Zambian government) and Non-Ferrous Metals Corporation Africa (NFCA), a subsidiary of the powerful state-owned China Non-ferrous Metal and Mining Company (CNMC).[4] NFCA owns the Chambishi mine, which is effectively the first Chinese-owned mining site overseas. Dormant since 1988, the Chambishi mine was taken over by a Chinese investor in 1998 for $20 million, and it paid for an 85% share (ZCCM holds a 15% stake in the company). The Chambishi mine has been heavily recapitalised, with $150 million in fresh investment. This mine is increasingly substantial, both in terms of copper production (50,000 tonnes) and employment (about 2,000 workers).

Other mining companies of Chinese origin include the Tycoon Mining Group, Central African Mining and Zanmeng. Recently there have also been a series of acquisitions conducted by Chinese companies involving local mining firms struggling with the negative impact of the global economic downturn on copper prices. The Jinchuan Mining Group took over the Albidon Mining Company (Zambia's only nickel mine) by acquiring a 51% majority of shares. The other firm, CNMC, bought out the Luanshya Copper Mine (LCM), a joint venture of the Bein Stein Resources Group (BSRG) and International Mineral Resources (IMR). The acquisition also resulted from the falling prices of copper, which made the previous Swiss and Israeli owners (the company is registered in the Netherlands) reassess their business prospects and eventually pull out. The Baluba mine was lavishly reopened on 22 December 2009. Chinese firms also own the coal-mining operations Collum Coal Mining at Choma, in the south of Zambia, and a manganese mine at Kabwe. Note that the latter was shut down indefinitely in 2007 by Zambian authorities due to high air pollution.

The mining sector is of utmost importance for both Zambia and China. Nonetheless, for Zambia it offers limited spin-off effects due to its enclave-type nature and few backward and forward linkages with the rest of the economy. Furthermore, the mining sector exposes Zambia to severe income fluctuations. Surges in copper prices or copper production may lead to appreciation and the so-called 'Dutch disease'. On the flip side, a plummeting copper price, as in 2008, pushes the local currency down, triggering inflation and forcing the Bank of Zambia to deplete its foreign reserves.

To a lesser degree, Chinese FDI is flowing into the infrastructure sector, where Chinese firms are building and rehabilitating Zambian roads and bridges, for example. Historically speaking, the very first infrastructure project concluded by the Chinese was the previously mentioned Tanzania–Zambia Railway. Other, at times very ambitious infrastructural projects, such as a 2,804 metre long bridge in central Zambia, followed during the Cold War period. More recently, the Chinese have pledged to build infrastructure for the Chambishi Multi-Facility Economic Zone (discussed below in more detail).

Overall pledges in the construction sector by Chinese companies have amounted to $44.7 million and the employment of 1,977 people, according to ZDA. The leading companies in this sector include Fifteen MCC Construction and Trade Limited, China Hainan, China Gansu, Mei Mei Investments and CBMI Construction. Chinese companies assert that their involvement in infrastructure has helped to reduce the costs of infrastructural government-funded projects by 30% (Yan Hairong and Sautman 2009, 5). From the development angle, Chinese investment in the construction sector may be beneficial for the Zambian economy in terms of employment opportunities. The potential for job creation, however, depends on the proportion of local labour utilised in Chinese projects. This is not restricted to large-scale projects, where indeed the benefits can be limited, as Chinese construction companies tend to import skilled labour from the homeland rather than train and contract local businesses. Rather, the benefits may be gained by smaller-scale local construction companies that are often subcontracted by the Chinese partners. There is also a growing number of small and medium-size Zambian companies operating in the sector that are controlled by their Chinese business partners which hold majority stakes, thus becoming de facto Chinese companies (Kragelund 2007).

There are increasingly more Chinese firms setting their sights on Zambia for reasons other than natural resource extraction and infrastructural products, although it should be equally stressed that their operations are still marginal in size compared to mining. Yan Hairong and Sautman estimate, for example, that there are half a dozen metal recycling factories owned by the Chinese (Yan Hairong and Sautman 2009, 5). They mainly deal in producing steel bars for construction and mill balls for mining. There is also an oxygen producer, a tire re-treader and a number of small copper smelters. The manufacturing sector is a central focus of the government of Zambia, which strives to divest itself of being overly dependent on mining revenues. This strategy is, however, not feasible as long as barriers and costs of doing business in Zambia remain significant.

The 'Chinese factor' in Zambian political discourse

Despite Levy Mwanawasa's victory in the 2006 Zambian presidential elections, the MMD's return to power was not the most significant outcome of the election. The emergence of the Patriotic Front (PF) led by Michael Sata (known as 'King Cobra'), and public support for this party, can be seen as one of the most substantial new developments in Zambian internal politics since 1991.[5] In terms of Chinese involvement in African internal affairs, these elections set a precedent that has been termed the 'loss of China's political virginity in Africa' (*Africa Confidential* 2006, 8).

Michael Sata's popularity has grown. This is problematic for China as Sata is usually viewed as a populist. Though the Chinese should not be blamed for Zambia's overall economic failure, corruption, poverty and bad governance, as they are the fastest growing and the most visible group of foreign investors, one can easily view Beijing as a symbol and source of at least some of Zambia's problems. Public resentment towards China was present in Zambia before the 2006 elections, and in the Copperbelt it was mainly connected to issues of safety standards in Chinese-owned mines (especially after more than 50 workers died in an accident at the Chinese-owned Chambishi mine in 2005, the worst industrial accident in Zambia for 30 years). Mineworkers' protests over delayed wages and the widespread use of Chinese labour in projects financed by China compounded the problems, while in the urban areas small businesses were being displaced by Chinese enterprises. Among other burning issues were the cultural differences and diverse work styles between the Chinese and Zambians.

The anti-Chinese sentiment led to demonstrations, which forced President Hu to abandon plans to visit the Copperbelt, 'due to fears that the workers would revolt again' (Hofstedt 2009, 88; Pant 2008, 38). The anti-Chinese mood in Zambia can be perceived as a form of political capital that the government was unable to use as Zambian officials welcomed Chinese engagement. At the end of 2005 Zambia ranked third, after Sudan and Algeria, in terms of China's investments in Africa; 10% of total Chinese investments on the African continent were in Zambia (Heng and Huango 2009, 106). The issue of the Chinese 'threat' then became politicised in 2006.

During the 2006 election campaign, Michael Sata straightforwardly criticised the Chinese economic engagement in Zambia. He presented China as an important actor in the present struggle for the exploitation of Africa's mineral resources.[6] Anti-Chinese rhetoric was not the most important factor that pushed Chinese officials into action, however. Michael Sata campaigned with the slogan 'Zambia for Zambians', and promised to expel Chinese businessmen living in Zambia (calling them 'infestors' instead of investors) (Corkin 2008, 148), together with other foreigners who harmed Zambian workers. But the most burning issue seems to be Sata's statement calling Taiwan a sovereign state. It was assumed that after being elected he would recognise Taiwan. At this very point of the election campaign, the Chinese ambassador in Lusaka, Li Baodong, threatened to cut diplomatic relations with Zambia if Sata won the election. Li Baodong's statement was a clear violation of the idea of the Five Principles of Peaceful Co-existence. Li Baodong's statement let the opposition present the Chinese presence as a primary cause of Zambia's poor performance, and revitalised the old narration of the struggle for independence. Michael Sata lost the election, but received the majority of votes in two populous urban areas where the Chinese presence in the Zambian economy is strong – the Copperbelt and Lusaka (Larmer and Fraser 2007, 612). After the announcement of the election results, riots broke out in Sata's strongholds. The King Cobra's supporters especially targeted Chinese-owned shops.

The usage of anti-Chinese rhetoric in Sub-Saharan Africa, and the real threat that politicians similar to Sata might one day take power in Zambia, forced Beijing to adopt a new political line. In 2007, President Hu Jintao paid a three-day visit to Zambia during his eight-state African tour. The length of the visit was seen as a confirmation of China's interest in deepening relations with Zambia (Davies 2008, 143). President Hu announced, during this visit, that the first Special Economic Zone based on Chinese experience would be launched in Zambia, and he promised tax concessions for Chinese enterprises. At the same time, the Chinese leader was forced to cancel his planned visit to the Copperbelt due to the post-2006 election growth of anti-Chinese sentiments and the real threat of anti-Chinese demonstrations.

The claims about the relative success of the strategy of anti-Chinese rhetoric in the Zambian political process have to be seen in the broader context of a lack of belief in democracy in the country. The voter turnouts are low, and according to the Afrobarometer surveys from 2006, 60% of Zambians were certain that the members of Parliament did not reflect the views of the voters. Nearly 70% of the population were shown to be dissatisfied with the state of Zambian democracy.

Indeed, the 2006 election campaign showed that the government's optimism regarding the Chinese presence in Zambia was not shared by a significant number of Zambians. The dogma of the mutually beneficial co-operation between African states and China was challenged, and the old rhetoric of plundering a nation's natural resources, as well as dependence on external powers, and a structural inability to create enough employment for Zambians, returned to the political discourse in the context of widespread unrest. The experience of the 2006 election campaign created an immaterial structure of Chinese perception on the African continent. This situation was also new for the Chinese, who started to promise more incentives, rather than the sort of messages contained in Li Baodong's threats. One of the most prominent examples was the Multi-Facility Economic Zone.

Conclusion

China and Zambia share a long history of collaboration during the Cold War period. The construction of the TANZAM railway, together with Beijing's support during the anti-apartheid campaign, play a mythical role in official bilateral relations, and are used as an exemplification of the win-win outcomes of past co-operation. Although Chinese capital does not hold the dominant position on the Zambian market, the increase in Beijing's interest in various sectors of the Zambian economy is a visible trend. One must take into account that the privatisation of the mining industry, enforced by international financial institutions, compromised the balance of the Zambian political system. The publicly owned sectors of the Zambian economy, with a special emphasis on the mining industry, as well as control over public administration based on client-patron relations, constitute political resources used by the ruling party in order to maintain its privileged position in the political system. With the growing heterogeneity of FDI in Zambia, a return to a one-party state is becoming less and less likely. Nonetheless, anti-Chinese sentiments, intensified by reports about 'starvation wages' and poor safety conditions in Chinese-owned industries, have become an easily accessible political asset in the two major urban areas in Zambia, the Copperbelt and Lusaka. Michael Sata has quite successfully filled a niche on the political scene by a combination of anti-Chinese rhetoric and criticism of the government's ineptitude. Instead of posing questions about the validity of anti-Chinese rhetoric, one should rather ask why someone like Sata appeared in Zambian politics in 2006.

Among many myths surrounding the scale of the Chinese presence in Zambia, the exact number of Chinese migrants is one of the most contentious. While Sata's Patriotic Front uses a scare number of 80,000 Chinese residents living within the borders of Zambia (Sata 2007), according to more realistic estimations, there are fewer than 6,000 (Yan Hairong and Sautman 2009, 4), and the government claims that it has given only 2,340 work permits for Chinese citizens. While the Western media zealously concentrates on accidents in Chinese-owned mines or the shutting down of Chinese-owned enterprises in Zambia, they are not particularly keen to shed light on less attention-grabbing but equally interesting features of China's presence. These, for instance, include the decision of the Chinese management to keep its 2,000 workers employed in Chambishi (Yan Hairong and Sautman 2009, 5) at a time when copper prices plummeted by 67% from $8,985.00 per tonne in July 2008, to $2,902.00 per tonne in December 2008.

The violation of the non-interference principle by Li Boadong during the 2006 presidential election can be seen in the broad context of Beijing's activity in the region. In December 2006, while speaking about the increase of cheap Chinese textile exports, South African President Thabo Mbeki warned that Africa might become an economic colony of China. However, in the vast majority of official statements the presence of Chinese investors is presented as a mutually beneficial phenomenon in African politics, and the leaders pledge to continue strengthening Sino-African relations. It might be assumed that the controversial declarations of Sata about the possible recognition of Taiwan and the deportation of all foreigners from Zambia have surprised Chinese officials, who have not met with a positive social response to the anti-Chinese statements in Africa. Aversion to foreigners was present during the

2008 elections in the Patriotic Front's campaign, but it was not at the centre of the political agenda.

Generally, it is possible to distinguish six features of the Chinese engagement in Zambia. Firstly, there is a long history of Sino-Zambian relations, and a common struggle against apartheid. China's lack of colonial legacy as well as Beijing's engagement in the TAZARA project may act as a solid base for the development of future relations and to some degree Sino-Zambian relations are path-dependent. Secondly, Sino-Zambian relations can be seen in the broad context of China's engagement in Africa. Thirdly, the MMD government supports Chinese FDI, and perceives it as an alternative and concessionary source of capital. Fourthly, Zambia is the third largest recipient of Chinese foreign direct investments (after Sudan and Angola) in sub-Saharan Africa, and the growing Chinese presence may create social dissatisfaction due to a clash of work ethos, cultural differences, and further accusations of 'Sino-colonialism'. Fifthly, anti-Chinese sentiments are the strongest in urban areas, and the Copperbelt province and Lusaka have always had a special meaning in Zambian politics, partly because of the relatively ease with which political agitation can be mobilised when compared with rural areas. Lastly, the violation of the non-interference principle by the Chinese ambassador during the election campaign in 2006 had no negative effects on official Sino-Zambian relations.

Notes

1. Copper is one of the colours of the Zambian national flag, and the national football team is often called the 'copper bullets' because until the 1990s players used to wear copper-coloured jerseys.
2. Kenneth Kaunda was the first among five African leaders who were honoured with the China–Africa Friendship Award in November 2009.
3. This is close to the peak of production of 750,000 in 1973, i.e. several years after the mining industry was nationalised.
4. As disclosed by government officials, the investment of the Zhougui Mining Group will reach the staggering amount of $US 3.6 billion.
5. Michael Sata is a former National Secretary of MMD. He left the Party in 2001 when Levy Patrick Mwanawasa was announced MMD presidential candidate instead of Frederic Chiluba who, supported by Sata, wanted MMD to accept a 'third term' for Chiluba's approach. After leaving MMD, Sata announced that he would run for presidency himself under a new party – the Patriotic Front. In 2001 the Patriotic Front won just 2% of the votes and one seat in the Parliament (Larmer and Fraser 2007, 624).
6. In 2007, during a speech to the Harvard University Committee on Human Rights Studies, Sata stated: 'The large-scale mining and construction firms have created industrial disharmony, due to providing poor working conditions which do not comply with labour laws, environmental regulations and occupational health and safety standards. They also pay 'slave wages'. The Chinese investments have also created only a limited number of skilled and unskilled jobs for Zambians, because most technical and managerial positions, as well as a significant number of unskilled jobs, are reserved for and held by Chinese workers, who have come along with the investment. The situation is worsened by disparities in wages paid to Chinese and Zambian workers doing the same jobs, with the Chinese being paid substantially more. Similarly, the issuance of work permits in Zambia is now marred by discrimination, because whereas the Chinese firms can take into Zambia any number of Chinese workers they wish, whether skilled or unskilled, the non-Chinese employers find it very difficult to obtain work permits even for very few skilled workers from other countries. Due to the favourable treatment given to the Chinese by the Immigration service, there are currently more than 80,000 Chinese nationals in Zambia' (Sata 2007).

Note on contributors

Dominik Kopiński is assistant professor in the Institute of International Studies at the University of Wroclaw, Poland. He graduated with an MA in management from the Wroclaw University of Economics in 2002, where he obtained a PhD in Economics in 2007. His research interests focus on the theory and politics of foreign aid, economic development and natural resource policies in developing countries. His academic interests focus on sub-Saharan Africa. Kopinski co-ordinates Fatal Transactions (www.fataltransactions.org), an international project that concentrates on negative aspects of resource exploitation in Africa.

Andrzej Polus received an MA from the University of Wroclaw in 2004 and a PhD from the same University in 2008. He is the author of over 20 publications and his major field of interest covers theories of international relations, decolonisation processes, the foreign policy of the UK and sub-Saharan Africa. Since 2008 he has worked as an assistant professor in the Institute of International Studies, University of Wroclaw.

References

Africa Confidential. 2006. A bull in China's shop. *Africa Confidential* 47, 18.
Agence France-Presse. 2006. Zambia closes Chinese mine over air pollution. *Agence France-Presse*. May 5.
Burnell, P. 2001. Taking stock of democracy in Zambia. In *Democracy and political change in the 'third world'*, ed. J. Haynes, 132–51. London: Routledge.
Corkin, L. 2008. China's strategic infrastructural investments in Africa. In *China's new role in Africa and the south. A search for a new perspective*, ed. D.-G. Guerrero and F. Manji, 134–50. Cape Town, Nairobi and Oxford: Fahamu.
Craig, J. 2001. Putting privatisation into practice: The case of Zambia Consolidated Copper Mines Limited. *Journal of Modern African Studies* 39, no. 3: 389–410.
Davies, M.J. 2008. Special economic zones: China's developmental model comes to Africa. In *China into Africa. Trade, aid, and influence*, ed. R.I. Rotberg, 137–44. Washington: Brookings.
Fraser, A. 2009. Zambia: Back to thef. In *The politics of aid. African strategies for dealing with donors*, ed. L. Whitfield, 89–102. Oxford: Oxford University Press.
Hairong, Y., and B. Sautman. 2009. Chinese activities in Zambia: More than just mining. *The China Monitor* 44: 4–7.
Heng, J.Y.S., and S. Huango. 2009. China's African policy in the post-Cold War Era. *Journal of Contemporary Asia* 39, no. 1: 89–115.
Hofstedt, T.A. 2009. China in Africa. An AFRICOM response. *Naval War College Review* 62, no. 3: 79–100.
Kaunda, K. 1967. *Humanism: A guide to the nation*. Lusaka: Government Printer.
Kragelund, P. 2007. Chinese investments in Africa: Catalyst, competitor, or capacity builder?. Paper presented at the AEGIS European Conference on African Studies, 11–14 July 2007, African Studies Centre, Leiden, The Netherlands.
Kragelund, P. 2009. Knocking on a wide-open door: Chinese investments in Africa. *Review of African Political Economy* 36, no. 122: 479–517.
Lanteigne, M. 2009. *Chinese foreign policy. An introduction*. New York: Routledge.
Larmer, M., and A. Fraser, 2007. Of cabbages and king cobra: Populist politics and Zambia's 2006 election. *African Affairs* 106, no. 425: 611–37.
Larmer, M. 2007. *Mineworkers in Zambia. Labor and political change in post-colonial Africa*. London and New York: Tauris Academic Studies.
Meredith, M. 2006. *The State of Africa. A history of fifty years of independence*. London: Free Press.
Momba, J.C. 2003. Democratic transition and the crises of an African nationalist party: UNIP, Zambia. In *African political parties. Evolution, institutionalisation and governance*, ed. M. Salih, 67–81. London: Pluto Press.
Mwanawina, I. 2008. China–Africa economic relations: The case of Zambia. Study commissioned by the African Economic Research Consortium (AERC).

Negi, R. 2008. Beyond the 'Chinese scramble': The political economy of anti-China sentiment in Zambia. *African Geographical Review* 41–64.
Pant, H.V. 2008. China in Africa: The push continues but all's not well. *Defense & Security Analysis* 24, no. 1: 33–43.
Ruffini, A. 2006. The revival of Zambia's copper mining sector. *Engineering and Mining Journal* 207, no. 2: 39–43.
Sata, M. 2007. Chinese investment in Africa and implications for international relations, consolidation of democracy and respect for human rights: The case of Zambia. Paper presented to the Harvard University Committee on Human Rights Studies Events Series, October 24, Harvard University, Cambridge, Boston.
Sautman, B., and Yan Hairong. 2008. Friends and interests: China's distinctive links with Africa. In *China's new role in Africa and the south. A search for a new perspective*, ed. D.-G. Guerrero and F. Manji, 87–133. Cape Town, Nairobi and Oxford: Fahamu.
Shaw, T.M. 1976. Dependence and underdevelopment. *Canadian Journal of African Studies* 10, no. 1: 3–22.
Shinn, D.H. 2009. Africa: The United States and China court the continent. *Journal of International Affairs* 62, no. 2: 37–53.
Taylor, I. 2006. *China and Africa: Engagement and compromise.* London: Routledge.
Taylor, I. 2009. *China's new role in Africa.* Boulder: Lynne Rienner.
Tripp, A. 2009. In pursuit of authority: Civil society and rights-based discourses in Africa. In *Africa in world politics: Reforming political order*, ed. J.W. Harbeson and D. Rothchild, 91–109. Boulder: Westview Press.
ZDA, 2010. *Chinese investments in Zambia.* http://www.zda.org.zm/246-chinese-investments-zambia.
ZDA, 2010. *Total FDI and Chinese FDI data – 2000 to 2009.* http://www.zda.org.zm.

Sino-Indian co-operation in Africa: Joint efforts in the oil sector

Karolina Wysoczańska

University of Nottingham, Nottingham, UK

> Sourcing sufficient supplies of energy to meet rapidly growing domestic demand is a major challenge for both China and India. The choices these two giants have made to meet that challenge in recent years will have long-term repercussions for the rest of the world. Although efforts to join forces in a global search for energy security are unlikely to overcome deeply ingrained Indian suspicions of China, both countries have already signed a series of energy co-operation agreements indicating the two states are seeking each other as strategic partners. This study provides an overview of the incentives for Sino-Indian co-operation in satisfying domestic oil demands. It will also examine the implications of such collaboration on regional and global orders.

One of the most significant developments in global energy markets in previous years has been China and India's external quest for oil. Their efforts to secure sufficient supplies have profound implications for international relations, with speculation that some of the choices made by these two countries may destabilise future world order.

China is now the world's second-largest oil consumer after the USA (Lai 2007, 519). The increased demand for oil and gas reflects the country's impressive economic performance, but also its lack of domestic reserves: China holds only about 2% of total world reserves of oil and 1% of gas (Dorraj and Currie 2008, 70). Until 1992, these reserves had been sufficient to provide for domestic energy needs, but since 1993 China has become a net oil importer and since 2003 it has replaced Japan as the world's second-largest oil importer (Bahgat 2005, 118). In 2006 almost 52% of China's crude oil consumption came from foreign supplies (International Energy Agency 2007, 168). This is the context for Hu Jintao, the General Secretary of the Communist Party, opting for a 'going out' policy that encourages the three main national oil companies (China Petroleum and Chemical Corporation (Sinopec), China National Offshore Oil Corporation (CNOOC) and China National Petroleum Corporation (CNPC)) to look for opportunities abroad to secure a long-term source of energy supplies (Dorraj and Currie 2008, 74).

India, due to economic growth and a much-needed investment in its energy infrastructure, is also facing the prospect of increasing dependence on oil imports. Currently the country is the fourth-largest consumer of energy in the world, accounting for approximately 3% of total global consumption (International Energy Agency 2007, 443). According to data from the International Energy Agency, India imports approximately 70% of its oil and more than 65% of its crude oil requirement is being met through imports from the (politically unstable) Middle East (443–95).

Some predictions indicate that by 2020, India will double its demand for oil, while China will increase its energy consumption by 150% (Roehrig 2009, 166). As the energy needs of both India and China increase, much current research focuses on a rising competition between the two giants and often concludes that cooperation among these countries is unfeasible (Cooper and Fues 2008; Scott 2008). These studies often indicate such obstacles as revolving around unsolved border issues, China's possession of Xinjiang and Tibet, Indian concerns about the ongoing relationship between China and Pakistan, and China's presence in the Indian Ocean, which has traditionally been an Indian sphere of influence.

Speculative research on Asia's future posits the likelihood of Sino-American rivalry in Asia and at the global level (Friedberg 2005; Mearsheimer 2006), with several analysts arguing that China's efforts to gain overseas oil supplies will undermine American national security (Klare 2001; Luft 2004). A prominent part of these debates is the role a rising India will play. Many who see China as a growing threat hope that India will be more engaged in international matters and help maintain the balance of power (Roehrig 2009; Richardson 2002). However, with co-operation between China and India increasing over the last ten years, it is necessary to sort out facts from speculation vis-à-vis the relationship between the two countries.

This study seeks to provide an outline of incentives for Sino-Indian co-operation to meet domestic oil demands, analysing the implications of such collaboration on global order. Although joint efforts in search for energy security are unlikely to overcome Indian suspicions of China, this study suggests that both India and China have their own interests to enhance co-operative ties. Both countries have already endorsed a series of energy co-operation agreements, which indicates that from now on, the two states see each other as strategic partners. The following sections describe several initiatives that Chinese and Indian authorities have recently undertaken to expand cooperation and also an overview of incentives to further consolidate Sino-Indian collaboration. The implications of increasing demands for oil in China and India on global order are then discussed.

Joint efforts to expand oil supplies

From a historical perspective at the diplomatic level, China and India operate according to very different practices. However, currently there is a growing awareness among them of global interdependencies and the need 'to make domestic political decisions more and more from a global perspective' (Cooper and Fues 2008, 296). China's foreign policy has to balance two main challenges. On the one hand the government's policy has to reflect national interest – social stability and economic growth – and on the other, the country needs to accelerate its integration with the world to 'melt away the suspicions toward China from the outside world' (Gu et al. 2008, 280). For its part India, since independence, has pursued global ambitions built not on economic power and military capabilities, but rather on presumed moral authority and 'traditional' values (Cooper and Fues 2008, 295). Now, however, India's diplomacy is moving toward compromises and trade-offs, based on pragmatic assessments of interests – as India's Prime Minister, Manmohan Singh, put it, 'Our relations with major powers, more recently China, have increasingly been shaped by economic factors' (Mohan 2005, 38). Trade between the two countries has rapidly increased over time (Qureshi and Wan 2008, 16–7) and by 2006 China was the number three destination for Indian exports and the largest source of imports (Asian Development Bank 2007, 234).

At times, Chinese and Indian companies have competed for control of oil fields overseas. For instance, in October 2004 China beat India's Oil and Natural Gas Corporation (ONGC) in Angola and in 2005 China again outbid ONGC to take over PetroKazakhstan. Yet China and India have also expressed a strong desire to join forces in a global search for energy security. In January 2005 India acquired a 20% share in the development of the largest onshore oil field in Yadavaran, Iran, operated and 50% owned by Sinopec, China's state-run oil company (Bajpaee 2005). A similar arrangement was struck in Sudan in 2002, where India's ONGC bought a 25% stake in Sudan's Greater Nile oil field, operated by the China National Petroleum Corporation (CNPC) (Scott 2008, 18). And in December 2005, CNPC and India's ONGC won a joint bid to buy PetroCanada's 37% stake in Al Furat Petroleum, a joint venture with Syrian Petroleum and Syria Shell Petroleum Development (Zhang 2006, 4).

In the same vein, both countries signed a Memorandum for Enhancing Cooperation in the Field of Oil and Natural Gas in January 2006. Besides pledging to bid jointly for crude oil resources overseas, this also encouraged co-operation in energy exploration, production, research and development (Lai 2007, 533). India's signatory, Minister for Petroleum and Natural Gas, Mani Shankar Aiyer (2006), expressed his view of such pragmatism: 'It is clear to me that any imitation of the "Great Game" between India and China is a danger to peace. We cannot endanger each other's security in our quest for energy security'. In 2008, further cooperation between China and India facilitated a contract in Myanmar where the China National United Oil Corporation (CNUOC), India's ONGC and South Korea's Daewoo International Group Corporation signed a 30-year gas pact involving Myanmar's three large natural gas fields (Lim 2010, 86). Finally, New Delhi has been granted observer status in the Shanghai Cooperation Organisation (SCO). Note in this respect that the United States also applied for observer status but was rejected (Roehrig 2009, 167–9). Though the organisation is largely seen as an effort by China and Russia to ensure access to energy and markets in Central Asia, New Delhi's new status in the SCO may allow India to further participate in economic cooperation within the region.

Incentives for Sino-Indian co-operation

The Sino-Indian quest for oil does not need to result in any notional zero-sum competition. Partnerships between both countries have already been manifested in the energy sphere and are likely to be consolidated over the next few decades. China and India's strategies and interests are convergent in many aspects, but they also face similar challenges.

Chinese and Indian companies, as late entrants in the global energy market, have to face the fact that Western powers have already gained control over most of the best available oil fields. Thus partnerships will make both states stronger competitors in the market and facilitate the search for potential emerging oil sources where

American and European enterprises are not present. With the volatile Middle East, where political conditions can easily give rise to temporary disruptions that would jeopardise energy security, it is understandable that Africa has become an attractive destination for both countries. Whereas the extensive network of economic and political relations that China has constructed across Africa has been the subject of increased concerns among policy-makers and scholars, it is worth noticing that to a certain extent New Delhi's approach to Africa can be viewed as driven by many of the same motivations as Beijing's: the quest for resources, new market opportunities, development cooperation and strategic partnerships. For example, both the Chinese and Indian have been courting Nigerian officials to explore new oil sources in hopes of reducing their reliance on imports from the Middle East. In 2008 state-owned Nigerian National Petroleum Corporation signed agreements with two Chinese oil companies to raise crude exports to China from 80,000 to 130,000 barrels per day (Konan and Zhang 2008, 393) whilst India agreed to a $6 billion infrastructure deal with Nigeria in exchange for extensive access to some of the best production blocs (Pham 2007, 344). More controversially, Chinese and Indian enterprises have jointly launched petroleum initiatives in politically isolated Sudan. However, it should be pointed out that China and India's options are limited. 'Chinese and Indian companies must look for oil where Western companies are not present and Sudan represents this strategy put into practice' (Alden 2005, 155).

Furthermore, between 2008 and 2012 new refinery capacity is expected to be built in China and India and while both countries have the necessary capital, they currently lack the technological capability to substantially upgrade and modernise their domestic oil infrastructures. For example, Chinese companies have been purchasing equity shares in established oil fields rather than buying rights for future exploration reflecting their relative dearth of technology and capacity compared with Western enterprises. Much of that technology is in the hands of American and European companies, thus China and India need close co-operation with the West in areas such as innovation, technology and environmental policy. In January 2008, Manmohan Singh called for greater co-operation between the two countries in the field of technological innovation: 'we have no choice but to widen our options for energy availability and develop viable strategies for energy security. We can do much more to jointly develop clean and energy efficient technologies through collaborative research and development' (Roehrig 2009, 166).

Rivalry between China and India in fact exposes their respective enterprises to losses and drives up the oil price on the world market. Chinese oil companies have historically been overpaying for equity positions and since Beijing has viewed paying a higher price to secure energy resources as an issue of national security, such bidding wars between Chinese companies and Indian rivals have further intensified such tendencies (Zhang 2006, 4). To date, Indian enterprises have been losing out in every deal that both countries have been seeking; Chinese firms have grabbed these deals by overbidding at least 10% more than Indian companies. For instance, in January 2006, CNOOC bought a 45% stake in an oil and gas field in Nigeria for $2.27 billion by outbidding the Indian competitor ONGC's bid of $2 billion (Zhang 2006, 4). Such bidding wars are raising global prices, which in turn have further consequences for both oil-importing and exporting countries. In that case, co-operation between Chinese and Indian oil companies not only brings financial benefits to both countries but it will also help to stabilise global energy markets.

Finally, China and India are searching for alternative oil transport routes and trying to secure energy sea-lines. Most of India's trade is by sea and nearly 89% of its oil arrives that way. For China, one of the major military objectives is to equally secure energy sea-lines in the Indian Ocean (Scott 2008, 17). For now, both countries compete for dominance in the Indian Ocean but growing Chinese naval capabilities to protect its maritime trading interests have triggered concern in both the US and Japan (Lei 2008, 139–40). As a result, the Chinese leadership feels compelled to develop a coherent strategy to alleviate anxiety over any possible naval confrontation. Since the Indian Ocean rim was traditionally an Indian sphere of influence, by building formal alliances with New Delhi, Beijing could reduce a potential source of conflict. Joint efforts would also of course improve the security and efficiency of energy sea-lines for both countries.

Overall, partnership will make both states even stronger competitors in global energy markets and will help bring down oil prices globally. Both countries have adopted an equity oil strategy, diversifying their import sources and trying to secure their sea-lines. Nonetheless, India and China equally have their own interests to strengthen co-operation ties, something to which we now turn.

The interests of China

As mentioned earlier, there is a growing awareness in China of global interdependencies and the need for greater integration with the world. American interests coincide here as engaging China globally to become a rational player which not only respects the international rules but also assists in maintaining global stability is in Washington's immediate interests. Thus a variety of factors come together to push China in engaging in co-operation with India, a major Asian democratic power, to establish a reputation as a responsible member of the international community and neutralise the view of China as a threat. Moreover, such Sino-Indian collaboration may also be an important element in a stable USA–China relationship.

China also needs to create a favourable international environment for its long-term growth. Thus Beijing has sought to avoid direct confrontation with other powers and develop greater room to manoeuvre (Ferdinand 2007, 857). In particular, China needs American and Indian acceptance to develop its naval capabilities and their cooperation to stabilise blue waters in order to protect its energy sea-lines (Lei 2008, 153–5). The Chinese leadership is also aware of the ability of potential adversaries such as the United States and India to establish domination over the Malacca Straits, which is a transit point for most of China's oil coming from the Middle East (Scott 2008, 18).

India is in a better position to maintain solid relationships with other major powers, particularly the US and Japan and this raises fears in Beijing of the possibility of a hostile coalition directed at China, especially after India's 'strategic partnership' with the United States, was announced in 2005 and strengthened in 2006. As one commentary has put it, 'the transformation of US–India relations has been one of the most significant developments in American foreign policy in the past decade. Both countries' leaderships regard a recent nuclear co-operation agreement as the most important step yet in their emerging strategic partnership' (Kirk 2008, 275).

The Indo-American alliance has rapidly become much more substantive in military terms than the Sino-Indian 'strategic partnership' announced in 2005

(Scott 2008, 13). Also the India–Japan–USA relationship is a far more promising triangle than the India–China–Russia 'chimera', espoused some years ago (Scott 2008, 13). Indeed, in 2008 India and Japan began co-operative initiatives in setting up energy efficiency centres and developing clean energy technology projects (Lim 2010, 83). Both countries also started collaboration in the development of the Sakhalin oil fields in Russia (Lim 2010, 87).

From a domestic policy perspective, one of Beijing's major objectives is to improve domestic companies' international competitiveness and establish the norms of a market economy. The Chinese oil industry lacks legal and financial expertise but is also without a clearly specified set of rules for such a market economy (Jaffe 2005, 278). Some progress has been made in reforming inefficient state-owned enterprises in the last 30 years, but Beijing is still not willing to renounce its control over the largest ones such as Sinopec or CNPC. The Chinese government's massively unproductive investment in the energy sector, and continued intervention in firms' management processes prevents Chinese oil companies becoming subject to market forces. It can be argued that changing this would strengthen their efficiency and competitiveness. India on the other hand, has a tradition of entrepreneurship and an advanced (albeit imperfect) legal system, that enables domestic companies to contest internationally with the best Western firms (Huang and Khanna 2003, 78). Although privatisation is proceeding slowly in India, the government has relinquished its monopoly over energy sector and allowed public companies to face competition. Therefore, an alliance with India would facilitate Chinese oil companies to familiarise themselves with the norms of market economy whilst also establishing a transparent set of rules and corporate governance systems.

The interests of India

India has particular incentives to increase its co-operation with China for searching for overseas energy supplies since almost everywhere in the world that the country goes in quest of energy, the chances are that it will run into state-owned Chinese enterprises engaged in the same hunt. As detailed, Chinese companies have been rather more successful than their Indian counterparts in the recent past. Until now, India has been losing out in every deal that both countries have been bidding for. As Manmohan Singh puts it: 'China is ahead of us in planning for its energy security. India can no longer be complacent' (Bajpaee 2005). Thus joint co-operation between the two countries can help India to satisfy its own energy demands and turn its biggest competitor into a strategic ally.

Although India is in a better position than China to develop profound relationships with the United States and Japan, China has been able to establish substantial economic ties with African countries. There is a significant presence of Chinese energy companies strewn across Africa that are involved in a variety of activities ranging from building pipelines to oil and gas exploration. Since it does not have the financial muscle of China, India has remained in the shadow of its larger neighbour. For instance, as India is trying to obtain a seat on the Security Council, it has courted African votes and China's support in the United Nations. Initially, China expressed support for India's wish but later Beijing withdrew their support and then pushed the African Union to also refuse to go along with Security Council reform with regard to the creation of additional seats on the Council (Cooper 2008, 300). There are clearly political limits to any notional Sino-Indian 'strategic partnership'.

India has also been concerned about an ongoing relationship between China and Pakistan, with Indian officials particularly worried over the Chinese presence in Gwadar, where China and Pakistan have built in co-operation a deepwater port. Gwadar is close to the Persian Gulf, where China obtains more than 50% of its oil imports, and the rail lines and roads from Gwadar provides China with access to the Central Asian market (Roehrig 2009, 172). For India, the Chinese presence may prevent New Delhi from maintaining the maritime regional dominance it desires in its own backyard.

The above analysis shows that India and China equally have their own interests for strengthening co-operation ties. However, it is axiomatic that India has much more motivation to enhance its collaboration with China. China's seat in the United Nations Security Council, its financial capabilities and its relations with African countries give Beijing a major edge over its neighbour. Nonetheless, China has to accelerate its integration with the world and attenuate the suspicions toward Beijing policy from other countries. New Delhi might play an important role in this process. Currently, China and India possess the weight and dynamism to transform the world economy and the increasing presence of the two Asian giants on the global arena will have many implications for other international players.

Implications for global order

Currently China and India pay more attention to the idea of joining the international arena, rather than what exact role they should play. They seem neither to wish to be a leader of a developing country bloc, nor to side with the developed countries (Gu et al. 2008, 280). Their foreign policies are driven by core national interests: economic growth, securing resources and energy supplies. The growing energy partnerships between China and India should not though be seen as a threat to any third party: 'the global energy market is well-integrated and energy policy should not be seen in zero-sum terms' (Bahgat 2005, 128). China has already been growing rapidly for almost three decades and there is little evidence that this is creating any serious imbalances in the region, or that China's rise is causing undue alarm. As Pranab Mukherjee, the Indian Defence Minister, has acknowledged, 'China's economic growth and economic strength is more compared with India's, but the impression that they have outpaced us in the region or on the world stage is not correct. They are playing their role and we are playing ours' (Mukherjee 2006).

However, the growing political weight of China and India in global politics will have ramifications for their relationships with developed and other developing countries. The biggest challenges arising from the emergence of China and India is surely for developing economies, but the impacts of these two giants are very diverse, creating both opportunities and problems. For instance, energy and raw material-exporting countries will gain from increasing trade, but at the same time will also have to deal with the impacts of rising volumes and prices of exports, thus in the near term, there will be limits for energy exporters to increase the rates of extraction of oil, coal and gas to meet the expanded global demand (Konan and Zhang 2008, 395). Chinese and Indian energy consumption will place increasing pressure on world energy prices and increase global pressure to seek out potential new oil fields. This will be particularly difficult for developing economies.

Conclusion

This study provides an overview of the incentives for Sino-Indian co-operation in satisfying domestic oil demands. It suggested that both China and India have strong motivations to enhance energy collaboration, since they share convergent strategies and cope with similar difficulties. Firstly, partnership will make both states stronger competitors in the global energy market since both China and India, as late entrants in the global energy market, have to search for potential emerging oil sources where Western enterprises are not present. Moreover, since the volatile Middle East could jeopardise both countries' energy security, it is understandable that Africa has become an attractive destination for China and India. Secondly, both countries need close co-operation with Western countries in areas such as innovation, technology and environmental policies to modernise domestic oil infrastructure. Thirdly, Sino-Indian cooperation can bring financial benefits to both countries and contribute to the stability of global energy markets. Finally, since China and India depend on sea-lines for their oil transport, co-operation on the blue waters would improve the security of transport routes.

This study also suggests that India and China equally have their own interests to enhance co-operation ties. However, India has much more motivation to increase its collaboration with China, than China does with New Delhi. Yet this growing energy partnership between China and India should not be seen as a threat to any third party. The global energy market is well-integrated and energy policy should not be seen in zero-sum terms.

Note on contributor

Karolina Wysoczańska is in the School of Contemporary Chinese Studies, University of Nottingham. Her research focus is on political economy and comparative politics, especially related to China and India. Funded by a Confucius Institute Scholarship, she is currently studying the Chinese language at Fudan University in Shanghai.

References

Aiyar, M. 2006. Asia's quest for energy security. *Frontline* 23, no. 3: 11–24.
Alden, C. 2005. China in Africa. *Survival* 47, no. 3: 147–64.
Asian Development Bank. 2007. *Key indicators of developing Asian and Pacific countries.* Manila: Asian Development Bank.
Bahgat, G. 2005. Energy partnership: China and the Gulf states. *Organization of the Petroleum Exporting Countries Review* 29, no. 2: 115–31.
Bajpaee, C. 2005. India, China locked in energy game. *Asia Times*, March 17.
Cooper, A., and T. Fues. 2008. Do the Asian drivers pull their diplomatic weight? China, India and the United Nations. *World Development* 36, no. 2: 293–307.
Dorraj, M., and C. Currie. 2008. Lubricated with oil: Iran–China relations in a changing world. *Middle East Policy* 15, no. 2: 66–80.
Ferdinand, P. 2007. Sunset, sunrise: China and Russia construct a new relationship. *International Affairs* 83, no. 5: 841–67.
Friedberg, A. 2005. The future of US–China relations: Is conflict inevitable? *International Security* 30, no. 2: 7–45.

Gu, J., J. Humphrey, and D. Messner. 2008. Global governance and developing countries: The implications of the rise of China. *World Development* 36, no. 2: 274–92.

Huang, Y., and T. Khanna. 2003. Can India overtake China? *Foreign Policy* 137: 17–24.

International Energy Agency. 2007. *World energy outlook 2007: China and India insights.* Washington DC: International Energy Agency.

Jaffe, A., and K. Medlock. 2005. China and Northeast Asia. In *Energy and security: Toward a new foreign policy*, ed. J. Kalicki and D. Goldwyn, 267–90. Baltimore, MD: Johns Hopkins University Press.

Kirk, J. 2008. Indian–Americans and the US–Indian nuclear agreement. *Foreign Policy Analysis* 4, no. 2: 275–300.

Klare, M. 2001. *Resource wars: The new landscape of global conflict.* New York: Henry Holt.

Konan, D., and J. Zhang. 2008. China's quest for energy resources on global markets. *Pacific Focus* 23, no. 3: 382–99.

Lai, H.H. 2007. China's oil diplomacy: Is it a global security threat? *Third World Quarterly* 28, no. 3: 519–37.

Lei, D. 2008. China's new multi-faceted maritime strategy. *Orbis* 52, no. 1: 139–57.

Lim, T.W. 2010. *Oil and gas in China: The new energy superpower's relations with its region.* Singapore: World Scientific.

Luft, G. 2004. US, China are on collusion course over oil. *Los Angeles Times*, February 2.

Mearsheimer, J. 2006. China's unpeaceful rise. *Current History* 105, no. 690: 160–2.

Mohan, S. 2005. Rethinking India's grand strategy. In *Emerging India: Security and foreign perspectives*, ed. N. Sisodia and C. Bhaskar, 32–46. New Delhi: Institute for Defence Studies and Analyses.

Mukherjee, P. 2006. India, China do not consider each other a threat: Pranab. *The Hindu*, June 14.

Pham, P. 2007. India's expanding relations with Africa and their implications for US interests. *American Foreign Policy Interests* 29: 15–23.

Qureshi, M., and G. Wan. 2008 Trade expansion of China and India: Threat or opportunity. *World Institute for Development Economics Research*, Research Paper no. 2008/08, February.

Richardson, L. 2002. Now, play the India card. *Policy Review* 115: 19–37.

Roehrig, T. 2009. An Asian triangle: India's relationship with China and Japan. *Asian Politics and Policy* 1, no. 2: 163–85.

Scott, D. 2008. The great power 'great game' between India and China: The logic of geography. *Geopolitics* 13, no. 1: 1–26.

Zhang Zhong Xiang, 2006. China's hunt for oil in Africa in perspective. MPRA Paper no. 12829.

The European Union and China's rise in Africa: Competing visions, external coherence and trilateral cooperation

Maurizio Carbone

University of Glasgow, UK

> This study analyses the impact of China's rise in Africa on the European Union (EU). Contrary to conventional wisdom, it argues that the EU's renewed interest in Africa is not the result of China's new assertiveness in the continent, but is a consequence of the EU's ambitions to become an influential global actor and the consequent search for a more coherent external policy. Africa, thus, represented an ideal venue in which different EU actors could simultaneously pursue traditional development goals together with new political objectives. Moreover, the existence of three competing visions within the EU negatively affected its ability to constructively engage with China: the European Commission sought to affirm the EU's aspiration to become an influential global actor; the European Parliament projected its preference for a value-based development policy, blended with paternalistic overtones; the Council of the European Union was driven more by the emotional reactions of some member states, who did not want to lose their position as Africa's main reference point. Unsurprisingly, the result has been a confused message, which China has found hard to follow, never mind Africa, since they were not effectively involved in the process and were sceptical about the whole idea of 'trilateral cooperation'.

'The battle for influence in the world between the West and China is not Africa's problem. Our continent is in a hurry to build infrastructure, ensure affordable energy and educate our people ... China's approach to our needs is simply better adapted than the slow and sometimes patronising post-colonial approach of European investors, donor organisations and non-governmental organisations' (Abdoulaye Wade, President of Senegal, January 2008).

'This has been a topic for a few years, yet we still don't have many things concrete on the ground. We remain open for the trilateral cooperation ... For the Chinese side, we have some considerations. If this cooperation is to become full fledged, it needs good environment; it needs mutual trust and understanding. But now, so many negative things, accusations, criticism against China. That is not conducive to our cooperation. We need to improve the overall environment. We have to listen to the Africans opinions' (Liu Guijin, China's Special Representative for Africa affairs, August 2008).

While in the 1990s Africa was neglected, since the early 2000s it has become a priority for both traditional donors, such as the European Union (EU), and (re)emerging actors, most notably China. The 2005 *EU strategy for Africa* and the 2007 *Joint Africa–EU Strategy* (JAES) renewed the long-standing partnership between the two continents, based on ownership and the integration of foreign aid, trade and political affairs. The EU–Africa Summit of December 2007, however, registered a number of disagreements between the two partners. By contrast, the China–Africa Summit of November 2006 was celebrated by both parties as the beginning of a new era in North–South relations; unsurprisingly, in Europe it was perceived (largely as a result of alarmist media reports), as a potential threat not only to the EU's relations with Africa but also to the existing development paradigm. While the EU and China apparently shared the same objectives – development, peace and security, ownership – their strategies were substantially different. On the one hand, the EU, seen as propagating North–South dynamics, supported a comprehensive model for economic, social and political development, with particular emphasis on human rights and democratic governance. On the other hand, China, perceived as promoting South–South cooperation, put forward a framework based on mutual benefits, principles of equality and non-interference in political affairs. Challenged by the newcomer in what it has always considered its backyard, the EU could no longer sit back (Berger 2006). The choice of the strategy to adopt was not easy because of the potential implications for the EU's ambitions in international politics, particularly the overall relations with China and the EU's approach to international development. Eventually, the EU opted for a pragmatic and constructive engagement, though the initial agenda was significantly compromised by a number of internal quarrels.

Against this background, this study addresses two interlinked questions. First, how has the European Union reacted to China's rise in Africa? Second, to what extent has China's new assertiveness affected the EU's policy towards Africa? To answer these questions, this paper is broadly divided into two main sections. The first reviews the road to the *Joint Africa–EU Strategy* to better understand how China figured in the negotiations and whether it affected policy outcomes. The second focuses on the proposal for trilateral cooperation made by the European Commission in October 2008 and endorsed by the EU Council a month later. For this, this paper is grounded in a review of primary sources (including drafts of key documents and speeches), secondary sources (including various journalistic sources), and a series of interviews (62 in total) conducted with officials and policy-makers from the European Commission, the European Parliament, five European countries, the African Union, four African countries, China, and the Development Assistance Committee (DAC) between May 2008 and September 2010.[1]

By engaging in process tracing, this study challenges the emerging consensus that China not only has triggered the EU's interest but has also re-oriented its policy towards Africa (Bach 2008; Tull 2008; Brautigam 2009; Wissenbach 2009; Ling 2010). If anything, the EU may indirectly have suffered from the fact that some African countries sought to use China as leverage in the negotiations with the EU. But this did not lead to a significant change in the EU's policy towards Africa, which in fact was driven by institutional dynamics and the EU's ambitions to affirm itself as a global actor. Finally, this paper questions the core assumption of the 2005 *European Consensus on Development* – 'a common vision on development' – in that it finds that the European Commission, Parliament and Council projected different views on whether to and how to engage with China.

The road to the joint Africa–EU partnership

It is widely accepted that the relationship between the EU and Africa has undergone major changes since the beginning of the new century. The most cited example is the Cotonou Agreement (June 2000), which 'normalised' the relations between the EU and former colonies in Africa, the Caribbean and the Pacific (ACP). The changes introduced in the economic realm – aid management and trade preferences – combined with a new emphasis on political issues – global security and migration, in addition to democratic governance and human rights – had profound implications on the nature of the relationships between the EU and the developing world. There are those who saw in it a 'triumph of realism over idealism' (Farrell 2005) or a shift from 'cooperation to coercion' (Hurt 2003), with the EU imposing its interests on weaker partners and using even the more normative aspects to impose its preferred models on developing countries. There are also those who saw in it an indirect instrument of structural power through which the EU sought to impose development and generic liberalisation rather than its specific interests (Holden 2009) or more simply explained it as a consequence of a normative shift, with old norms like partnership and obligation being replaced with such principles as liberalisation and democratisation (Elgström 2000). These features of an asymmetrical relationship were reinforced when the Cotonou Agreement was revised in February 2005 and in June 2010, with changes largely reflecting the EU's priorities, in vain resisted by ACP countries.[2]

The novelty since the turn of the century, however, has been the attempt to pursue a 'common' and continent-wide approach. This attempt to pursue a unitary policy towards the entire Africa, under the slogan 'one Europe, one Africa' was not an easy task. In addition to the relations with the members of the ACP group, the EU had developed formal relationships with North Africa through the Euro-Mediterranean Partnership (EMP) and European Neighbourhood Policy (ENP), and with South Africa through the Trade and Development Cooperation Agreement (TCDA). Moreover, EU member states had different priorities in their development policy, differences not easy to reconcile.

The process timidly started with the first EU–Africa summit held in Cairo in April 2000 and culminated in the 2007 *Joint Africa–EU strategy*, approved at the second EU–Africa summit held in Lisbon in December 2007 (Council of the European Union 2007a). At the Cairo Summit, there was an attempt to work together to achieve common interests, but despite the adoption of a Declaration and a Plan of Action it was clear that European representatives placed more emphasis on political aspects, notably human rights, democracy and conflict prevention, while African representatives concentrated on economic issues, notably aid, debt relief and trade preferences. The second meeting planned for Lisbon in April 2003 was postponed due to a disagreement over the presence of President Robert Mugabe and other Zimbabwean leaders. Because of the earlier imposition of a travel ban, the EU member states sought to prevent Mugabe from entering the EU area. African leaders perceived this as an inappropriate interference, arguing that it was not possible to hold a meeting without all the African states being represented (Olsen 2004; Sicurelli 2010).

Meanwhile, the adoption of the New Partnership for Africa's Development (NEPAD) had provided a platform for foreign donors and investors to work together in support of African development, while the setting up of the African Union (AU) had further reassured the international community that African leaders apparently wanted to take ownership of their future. At the European level, the EU's interest in Africa was shaped by the deepening of the integration process through the reinforcement of the Common Foreign and Security Policy (CFSP), as well as the European Security and Defense Policy (ESDP). Not only was it clear that the traditional means used to deal with Africa were no longer adequate, but that the EU saw its involvement in conflict prevention and management in Africa as necessary to become a significant player in international politics (Olsen 2008a; Sicurelli 2008).[3] Unexpectedly, some changes occurred at the beginning of the 2000s in the field of development policy. The joint commitment made by all member states to boost foreign aid – first in March 2002 and then in May 2005, when they also decided to allocate half of those increases to Africa – was complemented by an ambitious agenda on aid effectiveness, with the aim to deliver aid better and faster (Carbone 2007). Probably the most renowned achievement of these years is the *European Consensus on Development* (2005), through which not only did the EU attempt to project a normative vision of development policy – by referring to human rights, democracy, peace and security, partnership, political dialogue, ownership, and effective multilateralism – but, according to the EU's official discourse, also provided a policy platform setting out common objectives and principles of development cooperation for the whole EU.

With all these initiatives, the EU acting as a single development actor was certainly attempting to promote aid effectiveness, by avoiding overlapping between 27 + 1 aid programmes, while at the same time trying to strengthen its profile in international politics. The targets, though not mentioned in official papers, were the US and the World Bank (more than China), whose development paradigms were the dominating ones in international settings (Carbone 2007, 2010; Hadfield 2007).

In line with this evolution, the European Commission published a communication in October 2005, 'EU strategy for Africa: Towards a Euro–African pact to accelerate Africa's development', in which the central concern was the achievement of the Millennium Development Goals (MDGs). For this, the solution was to make aid more effective and promote better policy coherence for development. Peace, security and good governance were seen as preconditions to development (European Commission 2005). The latter view was emphasised in a paper produced by the High Representative for the CFSP, Javier Solana, in which the promotion of peace and security in Africa was seen as central to the CFSP (Carbone 2008). The European Parliament (2005) endorsed the idea of having a 'common' strategy towards Africa in November 2005, but strongly emphasised the need to use conditionality to promote human rights and democratic practices. The *EU Strategy for Africa*, formally adopted in December 2005 (Council of the European Union 2005), on the one hand represented a remarkable novelty by offering a framework for a more consistent EU policy towards Africa. On the other hand, it did not make a qualitative leap in that it reiterated existing commitments and positions. Two important points, however, should be made. First, the EU reaffirmed its commitment to support peace and security through the reinforcement of the African Peace Facility. Second, the concept of political conditionality was replaced by a support of the African Peer Review

Mechanism (APRM), a voluntary mechanism set up by African governments themselves (Kingah 2006; Schmidt 2008). The Strategy was criticised not only for its lack of ambitions, but also because it was agreed without adequate consultation with all stakeholders. On the European side, the drafting process was led by the European Commission and the British Presidency. On the African side, there was limited consultation outside the AU Commission. Because of this, at the EU–AU Ministerial meeting in Bamako in December 2005 it was agreed to transform the EU's strategy *for* Africa into a partnership *between* Africa and the EU (European Communication 2007).

Meanwhile, China's growing presence in Africa, particularly after the first meeting of the Forum on China–Africa Cooperation (FOCAC), in Beijing in October 2000, had brought new dynamics into the continent's relations with the rest of the world. When 'China's Africa policy' was published in January 2006 it became clear that its involvement went beyond development cooperation and trade opportunities to cover a wide range of sectors. Subsequently, at the third FOCAC meeting in Beijing in November 2006, the Chinese government promised to double its development assistance by 2009, provide more loans and debt relief, set up a China–Africa Development Fund, and offer more training and technical assistance (Taylor 2011). Probably because of the positive response of African leaders, Europe started to feel its pre-eminence in the region being challenged. For example, President Museveni, despite Uganda being one the darlings of the West, stated 'The Western ruling groups are conceited, full of themselves, ignorant of our conditions, and they make other people's business their business. Whereas the Chinese just deal with you, you represent your country, they represent their own interests, and you do business' (*African Executive*, 8 October 2008). President Mogae of Botswana also stated that 'I find that the Chinese treat us as equals. The West treats us as former subjects (read slaves). Which is a reality. I prefer the attitude of the Chinese to that of the West' (*ibid.*). The European sense of vulnerability was compounded at the fourth FOCAC meeting in Sharm El Sheikh, Egypt, in October 2009, when Beijing announced a new ambitious set of measures in the areas of development cooperation (including a major debt relief programme), trade (including preferential treatment for Africa's least developed countries), environmental protection and climate change, science and technology, and health.

A detailed analysis of the motives for China's presence in Africa is beyond the scope of this contribution (Brautigam 2009; Manji and Marks 2007; Steiler 2010; Taylor 2006, 2009). However, a few points must be made to better contextualise the EU's reaction to the evident rise in the 2000s. First, China's interest in Africa has certainly been driven by economic interests, with the aim of securing raw materials, gaining access to energy sources and finding a market for its manufactured goods. It has had, moreover, an important political dimension. By presenting itself as 'the largest developing country in the world', not only has China been able to project an identity of being a post-colonial actor, closer to the needs of developing countries, but it has also actively sought to gain African support for an alternative development model. Second, in line with the logics of its foreign policy, China has pursued a policy of non-interference in human rights and democratic governance. This has meant a rejection of any type of conditionality (except the 'One China' policy). This, however, has attracted wide criticism because of its (unintended) consequences, that of supporting undemocratic regimes. Third, Chinese development assistance has been to a large extent at odds with the aid regime that has gradually emerged within the DAC: it has failed to separate traditional official development assistance (grants and concessional loans) from other forms of development cooperation (non-concessional loans, equity funds and export credits); has undermined the existing system of debt management, by offering new loans to debt relieved countries (though this situation has gradually changed with China being involved in substantial debt cancellation); and has made extensive use of project aid and tied aid, thus aggravating the burden of aid fragmentation (Brautigam 2009; Tan-Mullins *et al.* 2010).

In Europe, initial perceptions of China's rise in Africa were negative. Newspapers and civil society organisations talked of a 'the scramble for Africa's resources' (Marchal 2007; Mawdsley 2008). Policy-makers, however, did not seem particularly eager to address the issue. For instance, in the context of the UK-sponsored Commission for Africa, China was only marginally discussed. The 'Communication of the European Commission' in October 2005, proposing a strategy for Africa, contained only some passing references (European Commission 2005), while the subsequent December 2005 *EU strategy for Africa* did not even mention China. The debate in the Council before the adoption of the Strategy, particularly the preparatory meetings, showed that member states did not have yet a clear grasp of the real impact of China's rise in Africa and were mainly basing their positions on what was being published in the newspapers (interviews with EU and European diplomats, May and June 2009). Of course, some member states, particularly the Nordic countries, were worried that their efforts to promote human rights and democracy would be undermined. Other member states though were more cautious, particularly the UK and Germany, and pointed to the fact that China was not a real threat because it lacked a policy towards the whole continent. Others, most notably France, saw in China a potential ally to counterbalance the new interest in Africa manifested by the United States (Alves 2008; Marchal 2008; interviews with EU and European diplomats, June 2009 and September 2010).

In 2006 there was a sudden acceleration in the discourse and following intense debates at the level of officials the issue was discussed in the context of the ninth EU–China Summit in September 2006 in Helsinki. China 'reluctantly' accepted to include Africa in the agenda, but this was welcomed as 'a positive sign' within the EU (interview with EU diplomat, September 2010). Beyond the rhetorical commitment to Africa's sustainable development and political stability, significant disagreements nevertheless emerged over the policy implications of any future collaboration, as seen by the joint communiqué:

> The EU reaffirmed its attachment to the principles of good governance and human rights, as embodied in its Africa Strategy. The Chinese side emphasised the upholding of the five principles of peaceful coexistence, in particular the principle of non-interference into others' internal affairs. (Council of the European Union 2006a)

The same type of approach was pursued in October 2006 when the European Commission (2006) released a new communication, 'EU–China: Closer partners, growing responsibilities, for a strategic partnership with China'.[4] Though the differences between the two parties were not hidden, it was clear that the EU wanted to have a 'structured dialogue' with China on Africa's sustainable development. Two points must be made here. First, the EU was trying to use transformative power: the invitation for 'transparency' on the activity and priorities of both sides was not so much a veiled criticism of China's failure to produce data on development assistance, but more an attempt to persuade China of its importance for aid effectiveness, in that it would ultimately help 'to improve aid efficiency, coordination and opportunities for practical bilateral co-operation on the ground' (European Commission 2006, 6). Second, by engaging with China as well as Africa, the EU was attempting to promote effective multilateralism. In this sense, one of the initial concerns was over China's preference for bilateral relations, whereas the EU had been instrumental in setting up the AU.

It might in fact be stated that the China–Africa Summit held in Beijing in November 2006 represented 'an alarm bell' for several European leaders (Huliaras and Magliveras 2008), as also witnessed by the preoccupation shown at the European Council meeting in December 2006 (interview with EU and European diplomats, May and June 2009). In the final communiqué, EU member states not only identified Africa as 'an area of key strategic interest to both the EU and China', but the sense of urgency was manifest in their intention 'to begin as soon as possible the structured dialogue on Africa with China', with the aim 'to create new positive realities on the ground' (Council of the European Union 2006b).

Meanwhile, starting in February 2007 a series of official meetings were held between representatives of the European Commission and the EU's member states on one side, and the AU Commission and African states on the other hand. There were also a number of public meetings and online consultations, though civil society representatives still expressed doubts about how the process of consultation had been conducted. This consultation process led to the adoption of the *Joint EU–Africa Strategy* at the second EU–Africa Summit held in Lisbon, December 2007. Some observers have claimed that the EU's renewed interest in Africa can be characterised 'as a reflex that is triggered by China's strong presence in the region' (Tull 2008, 7) and that 'China has become a factor in accelerating a process of re-orientation of EU–Africa partnership as its no-strings-attached approach provides African countries with alternatives to the post-Cold War development model' (Wissenbach 2009, 667). While there may be some truth in these claims, this point must not be exaggerated. Clearly, it was the European Commission itself (as a response to the presence of new actors in Africa), that argued that if the EU wanted 'to remain a privileged partner and make the most of its relations with Africa, it must be willing to reinforce, and in some areas reinvent, the current relationship – institutionally, politically and culturally' (European Commission 2007, 3).

However, China was instrumentally used by various interested actors, particularly some in the Directorate General (DG) for Development, to give more prominence to Africa in the EU's external policy (interviews with EU diplomats, May and June 2009). As stated by one official within the DG Development: 'The adoption of a new strategy for Africa was inevitable, and actually was part of what we have been discussing with the AU: we simply used the China scare to place Africa high on the agenda of the European Union' (interview with EU diplomat, May 2009). The Portuguese Presidency was also very active for reasons of visibility: its priority was mainly the successful conclusion of a summit and the adoption of a strategy under its term, also because the previously scheduled summit for 2003 in Lisbon had been postponed (interview with EU and European diplomats, May and June 2009).

Despite the promise of new initiatives by the European Commission, both the *Joint Africa–EU Strategy* and the 2007 EU–Africa Summit did not meet expectations. The preparation of the Summit, once again, was overshadowed by the debate over the presence of President Mugabe. While all Member States opposed the participation of the Zimbabwean leader, some vocally rejected the prospect of cancelling the meeting (e.g. the Nordic countries, Germany), while others (the UK and Czech Republic) decided not to participate. For their part, African leaders not only argued that *all* African states should be allowed to take part in the meeting, but also maintained that the Zimbabwe issue was secondary and that there were more urgent problems to solve. As a side note, it should be added that the exclusion of those countries that recognised Taiwan from the China–Africa summit in November 2006 did not result in similar righteous indignation from African countries or a sudden mobilisation for fellow 'victimised' African brothers.

Though the JAES and the accompanying 'Plan of Action' were the result of an extensive consultation process, (in theory) based on a 'Euro-African consensus on values, common interests and common strategic objectives', the dynamics in the negotiations were still those of an asymmetrical relationship. One of the most vocal critics was President Wade who argued that the EU was close 'to losing the battle of competition in Africa' because Chinese products were cheaper and Chinese companies 'more pragmatic' and better at carrying out business in Africa (*Euractiv*, 10 December 2007).

China's presence was felt in the attitudes of some African governments (Bach 2008). Nevertheless, there are no signs that the Chinese factor contributed to re-orienting the EU's policy towards Africa, as the EU managed to impose most of its priorities. For instance, the EU did not modify its pre-existing positions on foreign aid, the Economic Partnership Agreements (EPAs) and agriculture policy. The complaints of African leaders that European donors had not maintained their promises in terms of development assistance and that trade barriers and agriculture subsidies 'shamefully' protected European markets from African products, hindering their ability to trade as equals, remained unheeded (interview with African diplomats, May 2008 and July 2009). The EU was also able to impose both its normative agenda by emphasising human rights and democratic governance – 'a sort of obsession', according to some African policy-makers (interview with African diplomat, July 2009) – and effective multilateralism (by choosing the continental level of engagement, in spite of the limited capacity of the AU), and to pursue its security agenda, by concentrating on conflict prevention and management and on the control of migration flows. Indeed, the 'Plan of Action' included eight EU–Africa partnerships: Peace and Security; Democratic Governance and Human Rights; Trade and Regional Integration (including the implementation of the 'EU–Africa Partnership for Infrastructure', launched in 2006); Millennium Development Goals; Energy; Climate Change; Migration, Mobility and Employment; Science, Information Society and Space.

In fact, the launch of the two initiatives, often cited as being closely connected to China's rise in Africa, the 'EU-Africa Infrastructure Partnership' and the 'Governance Initiative', were due to other factors. The latter, by introducing the idea of incentive-based conditionality, was driven by the attempt to differentiate the EU's approach from those of the Bretton Woods Institutions, which was based on selectivity (Carbone 2010). With the former, the EU was building on one of the

European Commission's widely recognised comparative advantages, often criticised by non-state actors for not being directly linked to the achievement of the MDGs (Carbone 2008).

Indeed, the implementation of the first JAES 'Plan of Action' produced only new cumbersome institutional frameworks, with a large number of meetings and technical activities, often seen as the only indication of success (Bach 2010). In this sense, the expectations that due to China's rise the 'traditional donor-recipient relations will be transformed into a new kind of partnership ... designed to respond to global and regional challenges and no longer focuse[d] on a unidirectional – primarily charity-based – approach to development cooperation' (Berger and Wissenbach 2007) were not met.

In line with sociological institutionalist approaches, it can be argued that the EU's policy towards Africa has been mostly affected by the interplay of competing visions brought forward by different policy communities.[5] On the one hand, the development policy sub-system, mostly represented by the European Commission and particularly the DG Development, emphasised the role of poverty eradication, as well as the intention to strengthen the EU's common identity in international development. On the other hand, the foreign policy sub-system, mostly represented by the DG External Relations and the Council Secretariat, stressed political aspects with the view to reduce the risks of global insecurity and migration flows. Together with these institutional dynamics, we should certainly include the preferences of the member states, which supported one of the two visions, but also added a significant dose of emotional reactions, due to the fear of losing influence in what had always been seen as Europe's backyard and, to a less extent, the attempt to preserve some national interests, particularly in the area of energy (see Carbone forthcoming). In sum, China's rise in Africa certainly represented a significant event in the field of international development, but not a fundamental breaking point in the evolution of the EU's Africa policy.

The rise and fall of trilateral cooperation

In parallel to the debate on the strategic partnership with Africa, within the European Commission a number of policy-makers were more than eager to launch a policy initiative to directly tackle China's new role in international development. Of course, many observers noted that there were fundamental differences between the EU's and China's relations with Africa, but the initial misperceptions were gradually replaced by the realisation that the landscape for development was starting to change, and that there was a window of opportunity to transform bilateral relations (EU–China; EU–Africa; China–Africa) into a trilateral mechanism (Berger and Wissenbach 2007; Solana 2007). A number of options were thus examined: confronting; waiting to see how the situation evolved; dealing with it in the context of the EU–China strategic partnership; delegating the task to other organisations, for instance the DAC; or collaborating (Wissenbach 2009). The latter option prevailed, but the search for trilateral cooperation faced significant resistance within the EU, where different approach co-existed.

The first type of approach was that of the European Commission, though some clashes occurred between the DG Development and other DGs. Contrary to the prevailing views in the media and among civil society organisations, policy-makers within the DG Development, both at the administrative and political level, pointed to the need to constructively engage with China, though their motives differed. On the one hand, some officials using a political lens were convinced that 'soft' issues like development could be used as a starting point and would be likely to produce more results than 'hard' issues (e.g. trade and arms embargo). On the other hand, those who used a development lens maintained that any collaboration with China would ultimately be beneficial to Africa's economic and social development (interviews with EU diplomats, September 2010).[6] The Commissioner for Development Louis Michel, who also had a political approach to development, came onboard on the issue, as confirmed by a senior official in the European Commission: 'Michel took political responsibility for the issue, but the initiative came from civil servants within DG Development. He was fully aware of what was happening in sub-Saharan Africa, so it was not difficult to persuade him of the importance of engaging with China' (interview with EU diplomat, September 2010).

The approach of the DG Development has been characterised as pursuing a sort of 'functional multilateralism', which implies identifying concrete issues of common interest, rather than general concepts, and proposing multilateral solutions (Wissenbach 2008). A strategy that involved both public and private meetings was designed with the aim to 'build trust and persuade Chinese officials of our good intentions' (interview with EU diplomat, September 2010). DG Development officials met with their counterparts in the Chinese Ministry of Commerce and the Chinese Mission to the EU, as did Michel when he visited China in August 2007 and March and August 2008. A major conference was held on 28 June 2007 in Brussels, which according to an EU official was 'a breakthrough, because for the first time people from the three continents managed to talk to each other without yelling at each other' (interview with EU diplomat, September 2010).[7] The invitation of Michel for a *ménage à trois* – or to use less ambiguous words 'We are considered to be competitors, while, in fact, we are partners' (*European Report*, 3 July 2007) – was meant to steer China's increasing interest in Africa in such a way that it would benefit the region's development and prevent the EU from putting its strategic partnership with China at risk (*European Report*, 6 September 2007). The reaction of Chinese authorities was positive. Liu Guijin, the then China's Special Representative for African Affairs, indicated that his country was willing to play a constructive role, though he defended China's post-colonial identity as a donor and the principle of non-interference (*The Courier*, November–December 2007; *European Report*, 3 July 2007). Similarly, the head of the Chinese Mission to the EU, Guan Chengyuan, pointed to the fact that the two had different histories in Africa, but the rise of China in Africa should not constitute a threat to Europe:

> When China and Europe encounter each other in Africa, to the ordinary man it would seem that a collision is likely, and to the wise man, that this encounter contain opportunities. The crux of the matter is how to deal with this encounter. If it is not dealt with well, it could become a new point of friction between China and Europe. If it is dealt with well, then it could become a bright new point of strategic cooperation.

A setback in the process of constructive engagement was the resolution adopted by the European Parliament on 23 April 2008, which saw in China 'a competitor' and also urged the EU not to engage in trilateral cooperation if that meant compromising its commitments to human rights and democracy. China was accused of imprudent lending by increasing public debts of African governments, undermining local African labour markets by bringing in thousands of Chinese labourers, perpetuating gross violations of human rights and fuelling conflicts by investing in those African countries malgoverned by oppressive regimes. Beijing was also accused of doing too little to foster the development of local communities (European Parliament 2008; see also *European Voice*, 25 April 2008). The European Parliament's resolution blended references to the principle of solidarity with the EU's aspiration to be a normative power. The result was a comprehensive process of 'othering', with China identified as a major threat. In other words, 'it seemed like the EU was a benevolent donor and China was evil, who simply tried to undermine the good deeds of the West' (interview with international diplomat, August 2010). It also started a sort of blame game, provoking a virulent answer from the Chinese government, as witnessed by a note of the Ministry of Foreign Affairs: 'This is a highly irresponsible and unfounded accusation in disregard of the facts. We urge the European parliament to stop the confrontational and provocative act and do more in the interest of China–EU relations. No one is in a better position than the African countries and their people to comment on China's policy toward Africa and China–Africa relations. The African people welcome and support China–Africa cooperation, for it is in the interest of the common development of both sides' (*China Daily*, 25 April 2008).

Less virulent, but still critical were the reactions inside the European Commission: 'That resolution was an accident. Undoubtedly it made relations with China more difficult. But it was not appropriate for us to put pressure on the Parliament, because that would have been taken in a negative way. The Members of the European Parliament were influenced, probably too much, by the media, civil society organisations, and the evidence given by some sceptical experts during the hearings that preceded the resolution' (interview with EU diplomat, September 2010). Unsurprisingly, the tone used by Commissioner Michel (2008) in a subsequent trip to China was more conciliatory than the one used by the European Parliament: 'China has important and growing interests in Africa, including access to resources and markets and the deepening of political and diplomatic relations. These objectives are in no way incompatible with European views and priorities. In fact, they offer important opportunities for the African continent. China's growing activity on the continent is a positive force for the economic development of Africa, and that is a goal we Europeans share with China and many others'.

DG Development, however, had to face additional 'internal' resistance, particularly by the Secretariat-General and by DG External Relations, as well as the EU delegation in China. Their view was not to add another layer to the already complicated EU–China relationship: 'Within the European Commission, people were nervous on how to deal with such a sensitive issue; they felt there was a risk to complicate our relations with China. For this, people did not want to be too explicit about some of the most controversial issues, such as human rights and democracy' (interview with EU diplomat, September 2010). The initial plan to present a communication before the 2007 EU–Africa summit failed, and the official justification for that delay was that the EU wanted to concentrate on two ongoing initiatives: the EU–Africa summit itself and the conclusion of the EPAs (*European Report*, 1 October 2007). Meanwhile, the EU's dialogue with China over (and above) Africa continued, as confirmed by the discussions in the context of the November

2007 EU–China summit. In that context, the two parties registered the successful cooperation in the case of Darfur, and committed to find effective ways and channels of cooperation between the three parties (Council of the European Union 2007b). Interestingly, China seemed more comfortable with the idea of trilateral cooperation vis-à-vis its reluctance of November 2006 (*Asia Times*, 13 December 2007). Of note, European delegations in Africa were not consulted. This seems to confirm the idea that the proposal for trilateral cooperation mainly had a political dimension (interview with EU diplomat, September 2010).

By the time the European Commission published the communication 'The EU, Africa and China: Towards trilateral dialogue and cooperation' on 16 October 2008, most of the controversial issues had been deleted. The prevailing concern, in other words, seemed to be that of appeasing China rather than projecting the EU's interests and values (*European Report*, 16 October 2008). The memorandum sent by Michel to his colleagues in the College of Commissioners was in this sense clear: 'to demonstrate the seriousness of our intent but without going into too much detail or being too ambitious, so as not to scare off or antagonise proposed African and Chinese partners' (*European Report*, 15 October 2008). The Communication that was adopted by the College of Commissioners after an 'intense inter-service consultation process' (interview with EU diplomat, September 2010) proposed four broad sectors for 'pragmatic' cooperation on the ground with the view to enhance aid effectiveness and ownership of developing countries: peace and security; infrastructures and regional integration; management of the environment and natural resources; agriculture and food security (European Commission 2008). The choice of this pragmatic approach was criticised by commentators, who pointed to the fact that the European Union had given up not only on its strategic interests but also on its normative aspirations (*European Voice*, 16 October 2008; *Asia Times*, 28 October 2008). According to a European Commission's official, 'the final product was much more modest than how it had been originally conceived. Still, the general idea to start with a few concrete issues, which would eventually lead to bigger issues, was preserved' (interview with EU diplomat, September 2010).

The Council fully endorsed the proposal made by the European Commission on 10 November 2008 (Council of the European Union 2008). The surprisingly short interval between the two initiatives is due to the conspicuous lack of controversial issues from the final text (*Asia Times*, 25 October 2010), the cooperative approach of the French Presidency, and the general acceptance of the idea that confronting China would simply be 'pointless' and 'detrimental' for the EU and Africa's development (interview with EU and European diplomats, June 2009 and September 2010).[8] For a diplomat in one of the EU's member states, the general view that seemed to prevail was that 'Chinese co-operation with Africa is a major opportunity for Africa and there is space for both the EU and China in African markets and in supporting development' (interview with European diplomat, May 2009). It is also important to note that various member states (such as the UK, France, Germany, the Netherlands and Belgium) kept regular bilateral meetings with China on Africa's development (Tull 2008; Brautigam 2009) and did not have any intention to interrupt them (interviews with European diplomats, June 2009 and September 2010). Some pressure was placed by some European enterprises, particularly those operating in the infrastructure sector, but this was mostly done at the national level. Their major concern was that Chinese enterprises would be able to win all the contracts tendered by African governments through European budget support (interview with European diplomats, June 2009 and September 2010).

While the central objective of this contribution is to look at the issue from the EU's perspective, it is also interesting to see how both China and Africa responded to the offer of trilateral dialogue. For one, they did not show the same level of enthusiasm of the European Commission. In the case of China, the initial willingness shown in 2007 gradually faded away. First, there was still the perception that the EU was more interested in projecting its interests and norms, rather than engaging in true dialogue. Second, there was irritation at the conflicting visions coming from the EU, in that the European Commission, the Parliament and several member states did not share the same views. Third, there were concerns that a common approach with the EU would undermine China's distinctive approach towards African countries. There was also the conviction that African countries themselves did not welcome the idea of trilateral cooperation (interviews with European and international diplomats, May and June 2009 and August 2010). This scepticism was confirmed in August 2010 by Ambassador Guijin (2010):

> Roughly two years ago, when the EU was about to draft a document for EU–China–Africa trilateral cooperation, we asked our embassies in Africa to consult their host countries. The result was mixed. Some were enthusiastic about the idea, and some opposed it. For the majority it sounded good, but they had worries. They told us, we are working together so well, why make things so complicated, why make things more expensive. Because they know that their cooperation with China is more effective and the costs of Chinese projects are low.

Some policy-makers within the European Commission believed that the only way for the EU to really make headway was by first persuading African countries. That strategy was, however, never put in place (interview with EU diplomat, September 2010). In fact, EU policy-makers discussed on various occasions with their counterparts in China, whereas consultation with stakeholders in Africa was limited to the AU Commission, in line with the EU's attempt to strengthen continent-wide structures. Clearly, there was an overestimation of the AU Commission's ability to represent the needs and interests of African countries (interviews with EU diplomats, May and June 2009). Though the prevailing view was that the EU should not interfere in relations between China and Africa, at the same time there were divisions about the role of China in Africa, more than what had appeared publicly (Manji and Marks 2007; interviews with African diplomats, May 2008 and July 2009).

In general, however, African leaders tried not to get involved and this can be easily explained: not only did they resist the risk of becoming victimised by any new competition between powers (the analogy with the Berlin conference of 1884–1885 was cited by African representatives), but they also saw the possibility of playing donors one against the other as more palatable (Berger and Wissenbach 2007; interviews with African diplomats, May 2008 and July 2009). More generally, various African countries felt that some of the most positive traits of China's presence in Africa – new investment opportunities and aid with no strings – could be compromised by trilateral cooperation, i.e. European interference (interviews with African diplomats, May 2008 and July 2009). One of the most cited examples for these arguments was President Wade (2008) of Senegal:

When it comes to China and Africa, the European Union and the US want to have their cake and eat it. In an echo of its past colonial rivalries, European leaders and donor organisations have expressed concerns that African nations are throwing their doors open too wide to Chinese investors and to exploitation by their Asian partners. But if opening up more free markets is a goal that the west prizes – and extols as a path to progress – why is Europe fretting about China's growing economic role in Africa?

The policy initiatives of the European Commission and the endorsement of the EU Council paradoxically seemed to mark the end of trilateral cooperation. In fact, the scepticism of both African and Chinese partners was matched by the loss of interest within the EU itself. Momentum was lost because Commissioner Michel stepped down and several officials within DG Development changed job, and their successors decided to place their emphasis on other issues. Moreover, the rotating EU presidencies that alternated in 2009 and 2010 did not show the same level of enthusiasm of their predecessors (interviews with EU and European diplomats, June 2009 and September 2010). This was reflected in the fact that Africa even disappeared from the agenda of the 11th EU–China summit held in Prague in May 2009 (Council of the European Union 2009a). However, it was discussed again in the context of the 12th EU–China summit held in Nanjing on 30 September 2009, when the EU and China 'welcomed trilateral dialogue between the EU, China and Africa, and agreed to explore appropriate areas for cooperation' (Council of the European Union 2009b). Meanwhile, not only had China increasingly recognised that its activities in Africa implied the assumption of some responsibilities, but Chinese officials in development cooperation started to engage more directly with bilateral Western agencies (Brautigam 2009). Cooperation was thus taking place, albeit in a pragmatic and non-institutionalised fashion.

Moreover, new formal platforms were set up, such as for example the Heiligendamm Process and most notably the China–DAC Study Group. The Heiligendamm process, then renamed Heiligendamm L'Aquila Process (HAP) after the G8 met in Italy in June 2009, was started at the G8 meeting in Germany in June 2007. It involved the G8 and five of the emerging economies, Brazil, China, India, Mexico and South Africa. One of its key objectives was to foster dialogue on development issues, with particular reference on Africa. The China–DAC Study Group was set up in January 2009 following an initiative of China's International Poverty Reduction Centre (IPRCC) to provide a platform to share experiences and best practices. Membership included Chinese academics and government officials as well as representatives of several DAC members and observers (Belgium, European Commission, France, Germany, Japan, Norway, World Bank, UK and USA). However, it should be made clear that the European Commission did not engage in 'forum shopping', in that it did not willingly delegate to the DAC the task of socialising China into Western prevailing norms and procedures, though some argued that 'the EU's initiatives made it easier for the Chinese to engage with the West on issues of development' (interviews with EU diplomat, September 2010). At the same time, within the European Union the impression was that 'the China–DAC working group cannot be expected to advance the relationship as much as is needed, especially in view of the fast pace of change of China's presence in Africa', which ultimately meant that the idea of trilateral cooperation should be re-launched (interview with EU diplomat, September 2010).

Conclusion

This contribution has analysed the impact of China's rise in Africa on EU development policy by looking at the processes that led to the adoption of the *Joint Africa–EU Strategy* in December 2007, and the proposal for trilateral cooperation made by the European Commission in October 2008 and subsequently endorsed by the EU Council. Contrary to the prevailing consensus, it has been shown that the EU's renewed interest in Africa is not the result of China's new assertiveness in the continent, but is a consequence of the EU's ambitions to become a global actor and the consequent search for a coherent external policy. This has been in place since the late 1990s. On the one hand, the EU has been able to pursue its interests, particularly in the areas of security and migration. On the other hand, the decisions to boost quantity and enhance quality of aid have been seen as an indication of the commitment to eradicating world poverty. The two dimensions, it has been argued here, cannot be separated and Africa represented an ideal venue in which different EU actors could simultaneously pursue traditional development goals together with new political objectives. The growing presence of China in the continent gave some leverage to a few African countries in their negotiations with the EU, but the outcome of the December 2007 Lisbon Summit and the initial implementation of the *Joint Africa–EU Strategy* show that little has changed in the way the EU deals with Africa.

In spite of what the 2005 *European Consensus on Development* proclaimed, this study has also highlighted the existence of three competing visions and objectives within the EU which have negatively affected its ability to constructively engage with China. The European Commission sought to affirm the EU's aspiration to become an influential global actor; the European Parliament projected its preference for a value-based development policy, together with a paternalistic attitude aimed at somehow 'protecting' Africa from China's 'rapacious' appetite for resources; whilst member states were more driven by emotional reactions, for example, the fear that Europe would lose its 'legitimate' position as Africa's main partner. The result was a confused message that China found hard to follow, never mind Africa, since they were not effectively involved in the process and were sceptical on the whole idea of trilateral cooperation.

With hindsight, it can be concluded that there was a triple overestimation by the European Commission: that the EU would be able to act cohesively and to share similar objectives regarding its relations with both China and Africa; that China was a unitary actor (on the contrary its policy towards Africa sees the involvement of ministries, state enterprises and the private sector) and was willing to engage; and that, once again, Africa would be eager to accept what the EU had to offer. None of these scenarios proved to be the case.

Notes
1. To preserve their anonymity, I decided to code interviewees as follows: 'EU diplomat' for people working in the European Commission and the European Parliament (including

politicians); 'European diplomat' for people working in one of the EU member states; 'International diplomat' for people working in China and the Development Assistance Committee; and 'African diplomat' for people working in the AU and one of the African countries.
2. The major changes introduced by Cotonou were as follows: aid allocation would be made conditional not only on needs but also on performance through a system of rolling programming; new free trade agreements, the so-called Economic Partnership Agreements, to be negotiated and agreed on a regional basis before January 2008, would replace the previous preferential trade regime; the political dimension, which included issues that had previously fallen outside the field of development cooperation (i.e. peace and security, arms trade, migration, drugs and corruption) would be reinforced. The two revisions in 2005 and 2010, in addition to a reference to the MDGs, contributed to a further politicisation of the relations (e.g. combating terrorism, countering the proliferation of weapons of mass destruction (WMD), preventing mercenary activities, committing to the International Criminal Court (ICC) and flexibility in the use of development resources). On these issues, see Carbone (2007), Flint (2009), Holden (2009) and Holland (2002).
3. Since the mission in the Democratic Republic of Congo (Operation Artemis), the EU has been involved in a large number of military/humanitarian missions in Africa. On this, see Bagoyoko and Gibert (2009) and Olsen (2008a; 2008b).
4. For a review of the relations between the EU and China, see Balme and Bridges (2008), Fox and Godement (2009), Kerr and Fei (2007) and Shambaugh et al. (2008).
5. For a similar argument see Sicurelli (2010), who argues that the EU's attempt to promote African integration in the areas of conflict management, trade and environmental policy is significantly hindered by the fact that European institutions and member states project different views. See also Scheipers and Sicurelli (2008) and Farrell (2009).
6. In this sense, some bureaucratic changes are important to understanding the role of DG Development. The appointment of a new Director General, Stefano Manservisi, who came from the cabinet of President Romano Prodi, to replace Koos Richelle, who had been instrumental in the emphasis given to quantity and quality of aid, meant a partial shift of emphasis from a technocratic to a more political vision of development. Following Manservisi's appointment, there was a re-organisation of DG Development, and a new unit covering relations with new donors was created. In particular, one of the officials, Uwe Wissenbach, who had previously worked in the delegation in China and spoke Chinese fluently, managed to meet with various officials in China's Ministry of Commerce, as well as the Chinese Mission to the EU (Interviews with EU diplomats, September 2010).
7. The conference brought approximately 180 policymakers, scholars, members of think tanks and NGOs from China, the EU and Africa to discuss the issue. For a summary of the conference proceedings, see Wissenbach (2007). Another important conference was held in Shanghai in March 2008. For a summary of the discussions, see Yu (2008).
8. It is symptomatic that in his account to the British Parliament one of the development ministers endorsed the whole Commission's strategy and manifested reservations only about the lack of reference to unsustainable debt: 'This issue is sensitive, so the decision to omit the issue from a Communication which seeks to gain support for greater cooperation is prudent. However it is a subject of concern which needs to be raised, at the appropriate time, with the parties concerned' (See www.publications.parliament.uk/pa/cm200708/cmselect/cmeuleg/16-xxxvi/1617.htm).

Note on contributor

Maurizio Carbone holds the Jean Monnet Chair in the School of Social and Political Sciences at the University of Glasgow. His main research interests are on the external relations of the European Union, foreign aid, and the political of international development. At the moment he is working on a monograph explaining the evolution of EU development policy (forthcoming with Oxford University Press).

References

Alves, A.C. 2008. Chinese economic diplomacy in Africa: The Lusophone Strategy. In *China returns to Africa: A rising power and a continent embrace*, ed. C. Alden, D. Large, and R. Soares de Oliveira, 69–81. New York: Columbia University Press.

Bach, D. 2008. The European Union and China in Africa. In *Crouching tiger, hidden dragon? Africa and China*, ed. K. Ampiah and S. Naidu, 278–93. Scottsville, South Africa: University of KwaZulu-Natal Press.

Bach, D. 2010. The EU's 'strategic partnership' with Africa: Model or placebo? In *The Africa-EU strategic partnership: Implications for Nigeria and Africa*, ed. O. Eze and A. Sesay, 27–41. Lagos: Nigerian Institute of International Affairs.

Bagoyoko, N., and M. Gibert. 2009. The linkage between security, governance and development: the European Union in Africa. *Journal of Development Studies* 45: 789–814.

Balme, R., and B. Bridges, eds. 2008. *Europe–Asia relations: Building multilateralisms*. Basingstoke: Palgrave.

Berger, B. 2006. China's engagement in Africa: Can the EU sit back? *South African Journal of International Affairs* 13: 115–27.

Berger, B., and U. Wissenbach. 2007. EU–China–Africa trilateral development cooperation: Common challenges and new directions. German Development Institute Discussion Paper 21.

Brautigam, D. 2009. *The dragon's gift: The real story of China in Africa*. Oxford: Oxford University Press.

Carbone, M. 2007. *The European Union and international development: The politics of foreign aid*. London: Routledge.

Carbone, M. 2008. Better aid, less ownership: Multi-annual programming and the EU's development strategies in Africa. *Journal of International Development* 20: 118–229.

Carbone, M. 2010. The European Union, good governance and aid coordination. *Third World Quarterly* 31: 13–29.

Carbone, M., ed. forthcoming. *One Europe, one Africa*. Manchester: Manchester University Press.

Council of European Union. 2005. The EU and Africa: Towards a strategic partnership. 15961/05 (Presse 367), December 19.

Council of European Union. 2006a. Ninth EU–China Summit, joint statement. 12642/06 (Presse 249), Helsinki, September 9.

Council of the European Union. 2006b. 2771st Council Meeting General Affairs and External Relations, External Relations. 16291/06 (Presse 353), Brussels, December 11–12.

Council of the European Union. 2007a. The Africa–EU Strategic Partnership: A joint Africa–EU Strategy. 16344/07 (Presse 291), December 9.

Council of the European Union. 2007b. 10th China–EU Summit. Joint Statement. 16070/07 (Presse 279), Beijing, November 28.

Council of the European Union. 2009a. 11th EU–China Summit. Joint press communiqué. 10234/09 (Presse 147), Prague, May 20.

Council of the European Union. 2009b. Joint Statement of the 12th EU–China Summit. 16845/09 (Presse 353), Nanjing, November 30.

Elgström, O. 2000. Lomé and post-lomé: Asymmetric negotiations and the impact of norms. *European Foreign Affairs Review* 5: 175–95.

European Commission. 2005. *EU strategy for Africa: Towards a Euro-African pact to accelerate Africa's development*. COM 489, October 12.

European Commission. 2006. *EU–China: Closer partners, growing responsibilities*. COM 631, October 24.

European Communication. 2007. *From Cairo to Lisbon: The EU–Africa strategic partnership*. COM 357, June 27.

European Commission. 2008. *The EU, Africa and China: Towards trilateral dialogue and cooperation*. COM 654, October 17.

European Parliament. 2005. *A development strategy for Africa*. Resolution, November 17.

European Parliament. 2008. *China's policy and its effects on Africa*. Resolution, March 26.

Farrell, M. 2005. A triumph of realism over idealism? Cooperation between the European Union and Africa. *Journal of European Integration* 27: 263–83.

Farrell, M. 2009. EU policy towards other regions: policy learning in the external promotion of regional integration. *Journal of European Public Policy* 16: 1165–84.

Flint, A. 2009. *Trade, poverty and the environment: the EU, Cotonou and the African-Caribbean-Pacific Bloc*. Basingstoke, UK: Palgrave.

Fox, J., and F. Godement. 2009. *A power audit of EU-China relations*. London: European Council on Foreign Relations.

Guijin, L. 2010. About China-Africa cooperation, 30 August. www.focac.org.

Hadfield, A. 2007. Janus advances? An analysis of EC development policy and the 2005 amended Cotonou partnership agreement. *European Foreign Affairs Review* 12: 39–66.

Holden, P. 2009. *In search of structural power: EU aid policy as a global political instrument*. Aldershot, UK: Ashgate.

Holland, M. 2002. *The European Union and the third world*. New York: Palgrave.

Huliaras, A., and K. Magliveras. 2008. In search of a policy: EU and US reactions to the growing Chinese presence in Africa. *European Foreign Affairs Review* 13: 399–420.

Hurt, S. 2003. Co-operation and coercion? The Cotonou Agreement between the European Union and ACP states and the end of the Lomé Convention. *Third World Quarterly* 24: 161–76.

Kerr, D., and L. Fei, eds. 2007. *The international politics of EU-China relations*. Oxford: Oxford University Press.

Kingah, S. 2006. The new EU Africa strategy: Grounds for cautious optimism. *European Foreign Affairs Review* 11: 527–53.

Ling, J. 2010. Aid to Africa: What can the EU and China Learn from Each Other?, South African Institute of International Affairs, Occasional Paper No. 56, March.

Manji, F., and S. Marks, eds. 2007. *African perspectives on China in Africa*. Cape Town: Fahamu.

Marchal, R. 2007. The EU and China in Africa: opportunities and differences. In *The EU and China*, ed. P. Ludlow, 92–106. Ponte de Lima: European Strategy Forum.

Marchal, R. 2008. French perspectives on the new Sino–African Relations. In *China returns to Africa: A rising power and a continent embrace*, ed. C. Alden, D. Large, and R. Soares de Oliveira, 181–96. New York: Columbia University Press.

Mawdsley, E. 2008. Fu Manchu versus Dr Livingstone in the dark continent? Representing China, Africa and the West in British broadsheet newspapers. *Political Geography* 27: 509–29.

Michel, L. 2008. EU, China to join hands for Africa's development. *China Daily*, August 29.

Olsen, G.R. 2004. Challenges to traditional policy options, opportunities for new choices: The Africa Policy of the EU. *The Round Table 93* 375: 425–36.

Olsen, G.R. 2008a. Coherence, consistency and political will in foreign policy: The European Union's Policy towards Africa. *Perspectives on European Politics and Society* 9: 157–71.

Olsen, G.R. 2008b. The Post September 11 Global Security Agenda: A comparative analysis of United States and European Union policies towards Africa. *International Politics* 45: 457–74.

Scheipers, S., and D. Sicurelli. 2008. Empowering Africa: normative power in EU-Africa relations. *Journal of European Public Policy* 15: 607–23.

Schmidt, S. 2008. Towards a new EU–African Relationship – a grand strategy for Africa? *Foreign Policy in Dialogue* 8: 8–18.

Shambaugh, D., Sandschneider, E., and Z. Hong, eds. 2008. *China–Europe relations: Perceptions, policies and prospects*. London. Routledge.

Sicurelli, D. 2008. Framing security and development in the EU pillar structure. How the views of the European Commission affect EU Africa policy. *Journal of European Integration* 30: 217–34.

Sicurelli, D. 2010. *The European Union's Africa policies: Norms, interests and impact*. Farnham: Ashgate.

Solana, J. 2007. Challenges for EU-China cooperation in Africa. *China Daily*, 7 February.

Steiler, I. 2010. The best of both worlds: Some lessons the European Union should learn from China in Africa. *FRP Working Paper* 3.

Tan-Mullins, M., G. Mohan, and M. Power. 2010. Redefining 'Aid' in the China-Africa context. *Development and Change* 41: 857–81.
Taylor, I. 2006. *China and Africa: Engagement and compromise*. London: Routledge.
Taylor, I. 2009. *China's new role in Africa*. Boulder: Lynne Rienner.
Taylor, I. 2011. *The forum on China–Africa Cooperation (FOCAC)*. London: Routledge.
Tull, D.M. 2008. China in Africa: European perceptions and responses to the Chinese challenge. *SAIS Working Papers in African Studies*, February.
Wade, A. 2008. Time for the west to practice what it preaches. *Financial Times*, January 24.
Wissenbach, U. 2007. Partners in competition? The EU, Africa and China. Conference Summary Proceedings, June 28.
Wissenbach, U. 2008. The EU, China, and Africa: Global governance through functional multilateralism. *Studia Diplomatica* LXI: 69–89.
Wissenbach, U. 2009. The EU's response to China's Africa safari. Can triangular co-operation match needs? *European Journal of Development Research* 21: 662–74.
Yu, Y. 2008. Sixth Shanghai workshop on global governance 'China-Europe-Africa-cooperation: chances and challenges', 14–15 March. Shanghai: Friedrich-Ebert-Striflung and Shanghai Insitutes for International Studies.

China's 'soft power' in Africa?

Łukasz Fijałkowski

University of Wrocław, Poland

> Beijing's political 'charm offensive' in Africa has ostensibly made China a major player on the continent. The source of this success in China's African policy is sometimes seen in China's political and economic 'attractiveness'. It is true that China is building a positive image targeted to the audience in Africa, promoting for example the vision of 'win-win' mutual economic benefits from cooperation. This endeavour is close to the concept of 'soft power'. However, soft power is about dynamic relationships between an agent and the subject of attraction. Hence, the general growth of Chinese soft power and its success depends not only on whether China can sell its image to African states, but also whether African states are willing to buy this.

The history of Sino-African relations in the twentieth century is not long. Since the establishment of the People's Republic of China (PRC) in 1949, initial contacts were under a strong ideological influence and generalised Chinese vision of the world (Taylor 2006, 1–34). The significant change to this came arguably in the 1990s when, under Jiang Zemin, the separation in foreign policy and ideology was completed. Under his successor, Hu Jintao, China has sought to improve its security and underlined China's 'responsible' standing in the international system by continuing good-neighbour policies while expanding them beyond Asia.

The source of China's alleged success in Africa is sometimes seen in China's political and economic 'attractiveness'. China has put great efforts into building a positive image in African states, particularly through promoting the vision of a 'win-win' strategy of mutual economic benefits. This notion seems close to the concept of soft power, in the context of China's involvement in African affairs, and will be discussed in more detail below. The contribution is structured as follows. The first section contains a conceptualisation of soft power. The second section presents the different Chinese agents actively engaged in Africa. The third part focuses on evaluating the strength or otherwise of Chinese soft power in Africa.

Soft power and China

The rapid increase of Chinese influence and assertiveness in global and regional economic development and political affairs has opened the debate in and outside China (Li 2009; Zhang 2009) about a supposed Chinese 'charm offensive' and concomitant Chinese 'soft power'. The concept of soft power originated in 1990 through Joseph Nye's ideas on how to conceptualise the change in the United States' power. Nye stated that in post-Cold War global order, the changing face of power was most clearly seen in the rising importance of non-coercive tools of foreign policy, in the idea of how 'to get others to want what you want' (Nye 1990). This is a central theme in the concept of power, namely one's ability to affect the behaviour of others. For Nye 'there are three basic ways to do this: coercion, payment, and attraction. Hard power is the use of coercion and payment. Soft power is the ability to obtain preferred outcomes through attraction' (Nye 2009, 160). In other words, soft power is based on the assumption that an ability to attract others can change their preferences in a way that they act in the interests of the country projecting attractiveness.

However, the concept of soft power is far from unambiguous. The definition of power, one of the core concepts of international relations, can be understood from different perspectives. Thus, power itself is a contested term. The basic conceptualisation of power provides us with this definition: 'how one state uses its material resources to compel another state to do something it does not want to do' (Barnett and Duvall 2005, 40). But power could also be understood as the ability to make, receive or resist change. Nye, in his understanding of power, chose an agent-focused definition concentrating on the ability to affect others to obtain the outcomes one wants by coercion, inducement or attraction. The *attraction* element is the centre of the soft power concept, and 'convincing others to follow' is based on the appeal of one's ideas. However, as Janice Mattern points out, 'attraction is a rather subjective experience', which raises multiple questions about the nature of attraction (Mattern 2007, 98). Soft power then is about the attraction, but agents can control, as Nye argue, agendas and structure subjects' preferences so that some things appear attractive that might otherwise not be so (Nye 2007, 163; Nye 2009, 163).

The sources of soft power are the elements that differentiate it from hard power, and vary from traditional means of coercion and inducement to achieve one's objectives. Hard and soft power are like two sides of the same coin, both presenting the ability to change what others do, and they represent two kinds of power for reaching set objectives (Pelnēns 2010, 40). However, the sources of soft power are a little vague. Some of them are 'natural' in the sense of naturally attractive values, such as 'freedom' or 'human rights', but also they are based on the relationship(s) between different agents, in that they are socially constructed through reasoned persuasion. Also, soft power resources can be accumulated. In that sense, the state has soft power resources, namely innate cultural and ideological attractiveness, norms and rules. In this light, arguably only liberal democracies with developed economies could possibly possess the sources of and potential for soft power for others. Moreover, the resources actually producing favourable outcomes depend upon the context and skills of the agent in converting the resources into behavioural outcomes (Nye 2007, 164). This again largely favours developed states.

Soft power operates through attraction produced by 'culture (when it is pleasing to others), its values (when they are attractive and consistently practiced), and its foreign policies (when they are seen as inclusive, legitimate and having moral authority)' (Nye 2009, 161; Nye 2007, 164). Culture in this case is defined in the broadest sense and the nature of promoted values should be universal, while also presenting specific features of society and its way of life. In this sense, economic development can also be a source of attraction when it comes to the acquiescence of values embedded in a way of life. A successful economy is an important source of attraction. There are in general two ways that these sources are used for soft power. One way is the direct assistance of a country's government agencies to promote its culture and values, and explain its foreign policy. Another way is indirect, because it appears as a part of the social and economic by-product of the country's society (Pelnēns 2010, 40). Power defined in behavioural terms is about the relationship, and soft power depends not only upon the agent, but also upon the subject's role in that relationship.

Soft power was created by Nye as a descriptive rather than a normative concept and was designed for that purpose. Thus, its implementation could be limited in countries other than liberal democracies. However, the concept may be developed, although the difficulties of incorporating soft power into strategy have to be acknowledged. Firstly, in some governments the resources that can produce soft power are often dispersed among different departments and agencies and thus dissipated. Secondly, the role of the subject in the delivery of the desirable outcomes is more important than in the case of the use of the instruments linked with hard power. Third, the results of any action often take a long time to be evident. Fourthly, the instruments of soft power are not fully under the control of governments. Fifthly, soft power depends upon credibility, which can be easily destroyed by governmental action. Finally, in some situations soft power is simply not enough to deliver desirable outcomes (Nye 2007, 177).

With this understanding, China could be claimed to possess *limited* soft power. But the use of Nye's concept expanded beyond the original understanding of the term, adding also the economic instruments, broadens its utility. Chinese scholars interpret soft power, for instance, beyond cultural and ideological attractiveness, stating that the main sources of Beijing's soft power can be found in the Chinese model of development, its foreign policy, and institutions and agenda setting, which are gathered together by three aspects: cultural diplomacy, multilateral diplomacy and overseas assistance programs (Li 2009, 25–7). For such Chinese academics, it seems that everything except traditional military coercive measures are treated as a part of Chinese soft power. This is clearly problematic. Another problem is found in the nature of the Chinese socio-political system, where the state's control over society, however weakened since the start of the economic reforms, is still largely treated as a given. Thus non-governmental instruments of expanding the soft power's basis, such as the media, have limited possibility in increasing the indirect attractiveness of Chinese culture or 'way of life', given that is largely and fairly obviously pure propaganda and hence lacks credibility.

The surest way might be direct assistance of Beijing to its government agencies to promote its culture and values and explain its foreign policy. But with the proliferations of agents involved in the foreign policy agenda setting, it is much harder to sustain direct control over them in a coherent fashion. Governmental instruments of soft power are, in general, limited and hard to manage. In fact, most 'natural' resources of soft power are outside governmental control. So China can stimulate the growth of its soft power, but not necessarily control it.

Agency

Chinese involvement in African affairs in the form of a mixture of economic assistance, debt relief and expanding market access, is similar to the strategy of Western states, but as Bates Gill and James Reilly point out its uniqueness lies in the

Chinese reliance on the active involvement and co-operation of Chinese corporations in its approach to the continent, as a part of Beijing's 'going out' policy. The Chinese government promotes business ties with Africa by providing information, coordination mechanisms and financial assistance for Chinese companies and investors in Africa (Gill and Reilly 2007, 39). All together this often creates a more comfortable environment for Chinese companies than their own, more competitive, internal market. However, the Chinese government has had to face a growing dilemma in that there is now 'an increasing set of tensions and contradictions between the interest and aims of government principals – the bureaucracies based in Beijing tasked with advancing China's overall national interest – and the aims and interests of other agents – the companies and businesspersons operating on the ground in Africa' (Gill and Reilly 2007, 38–9). The gap between bureaucratic principals and corporate agents' goals are widening and there is already evidence of Chinese corporations taking steps that are at odds with Chinese government interests, creating problems for Beijing's attempts to promote a positive and constructive image in Africa. In fact, the increasing presence of Chinese companies in Africa is the source of growing popular resentment among Africans in a variety of states.

Thus, looking at Chinese foreign policy from the top-down could be misleading. The era of a lone leader who dominates foreign policy decisions is finished, accompanying the shift of power among the successive generations of leaders (Taylor 2009). Using the agent prism, information on agents can be incomplete and misleading, together with the expanding influence of bureaucratic structures, as well as non-governmental actors (Lanteigne 2009, 19–29). The different groups of agents pursuing their goals in their relationships with African states are diverse government institutions, together with provincial agents and corporations. Among the government agencies involved in Chinese policy in Africa, we can mention the State-owned Assets Supervision and Administration Commission (SASAC), Ministry of Commerce, Ministry of Foreign Affairs, Chinese lending agencies and banks, and also provincial and city governments. Thus the government's control over these agencies' actions is necessarily and increasingly limited by different interests and competition.

At the national-level, the Ministry of Commerce (MOFCOM) and the Ministry of Foreign Affairs (MOFA) are among the major players. MOFCOM[1] is obviously involved in foreign policy in Africa, where responsibilities are divided across four departments, each with their own set of interests. The Department of West Asian and African Affairs provides policy advice on Africa to top policymakers and encourages investment and trade, giving the information on local economic, political and social environments to Chinese firms. The Department of Foreign Economic Cooperation (DFEC) is responsible for regulating all Chinese companies involved overseas, including which companies are required to register with MOFCOM. The DFEC is responsible for the treatment of China's overseas workers by Chinese corporations. Meanwhile, the Department of Foreign Aid (DFA) plays the central role in administering China's aid projects.

In MOFCOM, the office of the Economic and Commercial Counsellor (ECC) is treated as a local MOFCOM representative in Africa, even though ECC offices are located inside local Chinese embassies or consulates and are subject to the embassy's administrative authority. MOFA focuses on political issues and advises Chinese leaders on foreign policy matters whilst helping implement China's foreign policy abroad. In the area of African affairs (which are bureaucratically divided into two: West Asia and North Africa, and Sub-Saharan Africa) there is close co-operation with the Chinese business community and MOFCOM. MOFA oversees all China's embassies and consulates in Africa, and oversees more routine, low-level decision-making.

SASAC is either the owner or maintains a controlling share of stock in any public state-owned enterprise (SOE). SASAC's main role is to maximise value and profit in China's SOEs, even if these companies' pursuit of profits ends up damaging China's broader diplomatic or strategic interests in Africa. Another actor is the most important Chinese bank in African policy, the Export-Import Bank (Exim Bank), which is the state-owned entity the Chinese government uses to dispense official economic aid worldwide, including to Africa, where it provides low-rate loans to African governments for aid programmes and encourages Chinese firms to invest in Africa through export credits, loans for overseas projects and international guarantees. In total, 80% of all Exim Bank loans to Africa go to five countries: Angola, Mozambique, Nigeria, Sudan and Zimbabwe. Province-level SOEs make up approximately 88% of all Chinese firms investing abroad, making provincial governments another set of key players in China's corporate engagement strategy overseas. Major export-oriented cities, such as Shanghai and Shenzhen, often encourage local SOEs and private companies to expand their operations in Africa (Gill and Reilly 2007, 42–4).

To encourage Chinese companies, Beijing has established ten centres for investment and trade promotion in sub-Saharan Africa, which provide business consultation services, special funds and simplified approval procedures for Chinese enterprises seeking to invest in Africa. In November 2004, China established the China-Africa Business Council (CABC) jointly with the UN Development Programme in order to support China's private-sector investment in Africa. CABC is a form of a public-private partnership. In 2002 the government began selecting some 50 companies from the most promising or strategic SOEs in China that have started to enjoy a range of benefits from the government, including information-sharing networks, domestic tax breaks, cheap land and low-interest funding from state-owned banks. Together with smaller enterprises, more than 700 Chinese companies are now involved in cooperative projects in Africa, mostly engaging in capital-intensive resource extraction (such as oil and minerals) and construction sectors (Gill and Reilly 2007, 40).

In Africa, China's top leaders have encouraged SOEs to seek out exploration and supply contracts with oil, gas and other natural resource-producing countries. In Sudan, 13 of the 15 largest foreign companies operating are Chinese (among them China National Petroleum Company and Sinopec), primarily in the oil industry. Sudan was an oil importer before the Chinese firms arrived, and now earns some $2 billion in oil export per year. Chinese firms are also involved in building transportation, electrical and communications' infrastructure, often linked with the investments in oil sector. For example, in Sudan China's Petroleum Engineering Construction Group is building a tanker terminal in Port Sudan on the Red Sea. In addition, Chinese firms are building Sudan's Merowe Dam, worth $650 million and a hydroelectric plant at Kafue Gorge in Zambia, worth $600 million. By 2005 the accumulated value of Chinese firms' construction contracts in Africa had reached $34 billion. Chinese companies are also involved in textile manufacturing, and in agricultural and fish processing projects. Together with the increased engagement of Chinese companies, the growing number of Chinese workers provide low-cost expertise and manual labour for Chinese corporations. The largest Chinese population is in South Africa, with other large communities in Algeria, Nigeria, Sudan and Zimbabwe. However, most long-term Chinese residents are small-scale merchants who sell inexpensive consumer goods, run restaurants and Chinese medical clinics (Gill and Reilly 2007, 40–1).

In overall Chinese policy in Africa, the government in Beijing is trying to ensure that these diverse agents will act along the general policy goals. But the government relies more and more on an increasingly complex array of government oversight agencies to accomplish these goals, and the ability to achieve desired outcomes is ever more difficult. In short, the multiplicity of Chinese actors with widely divergent aims and goals undermines any coherence in advancing a definite 'soft power' by Beijing. What these instruments might actually be is now turned to.

Instruments of China's soft power in Africa

Soft power as a concept is based on behavioural notions of power focusing on an agent's attraction to the subject. Communication is a key element for making sources of soft power work (e.g. through the media and those actions by which a country sends its message to promote its culture and values and explains its foreign policy). A government's public diplomacy is directed at an audience by influencing the content of information and the form of communication (Pelnēns 2010, 41). Thus, the instruments of soft power include various aspects of communication, such as the media, non-governmental organisations (NGOs), which share the broad state vision, a country's diplomatic services and policies, centres of culture, science, and education, and events through which soft power is broadly projected. However, a government never fully controls soft power, making mistakes, errors and misunderstandings possible. Also, attraction depends upon what is happening in the mind of the subject. While there may be instances of coercive verbal manipulation, there are often more degrees of freedom for the subject when the means involve soft power. Finally, power, and especially soft power, is always dependent on the context where power relations exist. For soft power it is important that the background conditions are not in contradiction with the aim to get attractiveness and change preferences.

China's government is devoted to sending positive signals to a wide audience as long as it serves well its foreign policy. Looking at the history of the relationship(s) between China and Africa in the post-1949 period marks the transformation of the focus from that of ideology and opposition to colonialism and American neo-colonialism and Soviet 'social imperialism', to 'one which has stressed mutual benefits, partnerships and trade, especially in energy and commodities. The Sino-African relationship has developed since the turn of the century into one of the most visible examples of China's growing confidence in cross-regional diplomacy, as well as further underscoring Beijing's commitment to expanding trade with developing regions' (Lanteigne 2009, 132). The White Paper 'China's Africa Policy' emphasises that the:

> China–Africa friendship is embedded in the long history of interchange. Sharing similar historical experience, China and Africa have all along sympathised with and supported each other in the struggle for national liberation and forged a profound friendship' and that 'enhancing solidarity and cooperation with African countries has always been an

important component of China's independent foreign policy of peace ... China will ... establish and develop a new type of strategic partnership with Africa, featuring political equality and mutual trust, economic win-win cooperation and cultural exchange (China's African Policy 2006).

The reasons for the growing importance of Africa since the 1990s for China were basically the desire to repair international relations after the Tiananmen incident, a growing interest in African resources and commodities, and China's growing self-confidence in cross-regional diplomacy (Taylor 2009). Beijing's lack of a colonial legacy in Africa was and is still very helpful for symbolical separation from the continent's other great power trading partners.

These aspects of Chinese involvement in Africa form the basics of China's policy in the region. This is especially the case after economic issues replaced the ideological fever of the 1960s and 1970s in Chinese foreign policy. Africa gained new attention in Beijing and the continent became a major recipient of Chinese investment as a result of the 'going out' policy. In 1996 the then president Jiang Zemin outlined China's 'Five Point Proposal' for Africa, namely a reliable friendship, sovereign equality, non-intervention, mutually beneficial development and international cooperation. For China, energy became the most important aspect of the growing economic linkages between the two sides. Seeking the opportunity to diversify its energy supply away from the Middle East, China perceives African oil and gas resources as an important factor, especially given that these resources are relatively underdeveloped. Special deals have been signed with Angola, Gabon, Nigeria and Sudan, and at current rates, Africa's share of Chinese oil imports may be as high as 30% by the end of the current decade (Lanteigne 2009, 134). However, comparing American and European shares of total oil production in Africa (32 and 33% respectively), China's share is still relatively small (9%) (McGiffert 2009, 30). The Chinese role though is arguably more visible in the regions where Westerns companies are reluctant to engage, for example in Sudan (Patey 2007). This, however, creates serious image problems for China in the field of legitimisation.

Based mostly on energy and commodity development, Sino-African trade has grown since the beginning of the 1990s and China takes 40% of total African exports to Asia, and accounts for more than one-third of Asia's total exports to Africa (Broadman 2007, 69–80). Chinese investment has grown significantly, with China's Exim Bank planning on investing $20 billion in Africa between 2008 and 2011.

However, stresses in the relationship highlights two difficulties regarding soft power. As was stated earlier, the application of the concept into political practice creates problems. The difficulty with state control over the instruments of soft power has already been noted, but also it is important to understand who is the object of the attraction. Is it a government or a country's population? Subjects of soft power are those countries, groups and individuals that a country is applying soft power to and is trying to attract, for example a country's elites, public opinion that represents the majority of a country's society and particular target groups. Considering the strong attachment of Beijing to state-protecting norms of sovereignty and non-interference in a country's internal affairs, and greater governmental control over official relations, the most likely first objects of attraction are the political and economic elites of African states. Experience regarding relations between government and civil society organisations is limited – at best – in China. Thus as

Zhongying Pang (2008, 136–7) has pointed out, the value gap between China and some African states is widening.

A successful economy is also an important source of attraction and Chinese economic success is a powerful magnet for some. African countries can claim to try to emulate the Chinese example, but in doing so also get access to the Chinese market for their own commodities. Many developing countries and international economic institutions (mainly the World Bank and the International Monetary Fund) have praised China's economic performance. This in itself, however, is not enough to construct a coherent notion of Chinese soft power, particularly as there are wide disagreements as to what exactly the 'Chinese model' is.

Indeed, though the most attractive aspect of Chinese strategy for African elites is its model of development, the source of Chinese 'economic miracle' is a hotly debated issue. And as Pang argues, China is reluctant to actually promote its 'model' in Africa, as an active promotion of the Chinese experience would be in fact in sharp contradiction to one of China's foreign policy principles, respect for other country's right to choose their own approaches to managing their own social systems (Pang 2008, 134).

In its political relations, China's diplomacy stress the notion of solidarity and South–South cooperation, and the fact that China has never sought to subjugate, colonise or enslave Africa. Chinese discourse also emphasises the notion of respect for African countries embodied in its support for non-interference and respect for sovereignty. Though this may very well attract African elites' appreciation, in autocratic regimes where the bulk of the population suffer from corrupt and incompetent ruling cliques, it is doubtful that China's power to attract is bolstered by support for the likes of Robert Mugabe, Ali Bongo or Paul Biya.

In the case of Africa, the primary evident tool of Chinese soft power is development assistance. However, it is hard to calculate real data in this regard as Beijing does not publish official statistics and because it remains unclear what percentage of China's aid actually qualifies as aid under Development Assistance Committee definitions.[2] Also, China rarely coordinates its actions with other donors. What is interesting about Chinese aid is that it is not generally tied to conditions, other than supporting Chinese investments. Also, China has no tariffs on exports from Africa's 25 poorest nations. Much of China's aid to Africa goes for infrastructure projects, something which is widely appreciated.

In the discourse over Chinese soft power there are statements abounding that China is becoming a 'cultural magnet' for many people in Asia. But this cultural attraction is extremely limited outside of East Asia. At best, China is mostly attractive in the economic field, especially with the growing appeal among some developing countries of a so-called 'Beijing Consensus' as a source of rapid economic growth, even if this notion is radically destabilised by empirical reality or conceptual fuzziness. Generally, in the discourse about China's soft power there is an absence of issues surrounding the legitimacy or moral authority of Chinese power and also whether there exists any universal appeal inherent in Chinese ideas, cultural, economic and political practices (Zhang 2009, 52–3). This is remarkable.

According to the 2007 Pew Global Attitudes Project, which in a sampling of African countries, Chinese influence was largely perceived as growing and as more positive than American influence. In Africa, favourable views of China outnumber critical judgments by two-to-one or more in every country except South Africa (Pew

Global Attitudes Project 2007, 41). This suggests that China's image is quite positive at the moment, but a causal link to notions of Chinese soft power is difficult to prove. As soft power is about relations and is based on an assumption that an ability to attract others changes their preferences in a way that they act in the interests of the country projecting attractiveness, it is difficult to argue that China projects soft power in Africa. Positive image alone is not necessarily soft power. It needs to be used properly by the agent projecting attractiveness, which in the case of China is not a simple task.

Conclusion

The Chinese growing presence outside of East Asia is a source of anxiety for some and hope for others. In general, China has become a more active actor in international relations, together with the growing importance of the Chinese economy for global trade. Still, it is not clear if China will be a status quo power or a revisionist state in the terms of the global order. However, it is sure that a new competitor for the United States and the EU in Africa has risen. Of course, Chinese engagement in Africa creates positive and negative consequences, and Chinese agents, often at odds with any official agenda, pursue aggressive economic policies similar to the exploitation of Africa's resources by other powers. At best, China's 'soft power' instrument in Africa is the appeal of its 'model' of development, and the idea of a new type of strategic partnership with Africa based on political equality and mutual trust – the scripted 'win-win' cooperation mantra. But different agents are involved in Chinese African policy, and the government's ability to ensure that these diverse agents will act according to the general policy goals is highly limited. The government relies increasingly on a complex array of government agencies to accomplish these goals, and the ability to achieve desired outcomes is complicated.

Moreover, soft power is about the dynamic relationship between the agent and subject of attraction. It is hard to evaluate the strength and scope of Chinese soft power in Africa, although it appears to be at best confined to the elites. The general potency of Chinese soft power and its success depends not only on the issue of whether China will be able to sell itself to African states, but also will African states be willing to buy it. In the context where the majority of citizens are radically disenfranchised by their own governments, the reach of any notional Chinese soft power in Africa appears very limited indeed.

Notes

1. In 1997, the State Economic and Trade Commission (SETC), modelled in part after the Japanese Ministry of International Trade and Industry (MITI), was created as a 'super-ministry'. In 2003, SETC was broken up, and some pieces were merged with the Ministry of Foreign Trade to become the Ministry of Commerce (MOFCOM).
2. Official Development Assistance (ODA) is defined as grants or loans to countries and territories which are: (a) undertaken by the official sector; (b) promoting economic development and welfare as the main objective; and (c) at concessional financial terms (if a loan with a grant element of at least 25%). In addition to financial flows, technical co-operation is included in aid. Grants, loans and credits for military purposes are excluded. Transfer payments to private individuals (e.g. pensions, reparations or insurance payouts) are in general not counted.

Note on contributor
Łukasz Fijałkowski is an assistant professor at the Institute of International Studies, University of Wrocław. His research interests focus on international security, the international relations of the Asia-Pacific, and the phenomenon of regionalism.

References
Barnett, M., and R. Duvall. 2005. Power in international politics. *International Organization* 59, no. 1: 140–77.
Broadman, H. 2007. *Africa's silk road: China and India's new economic frontier*. Washington DC: World Bank.
China's African Policy. 2006. *China's African policy*. Beijing: Ministry of Foreign Affairs.
Gill, B., and J. Reilly. 2007. The tenuous hold of China Inc. in Africa. *Washington Quarterly* 30, no. 3: 37–52.
Lanteigne, M. 2009. *Chinese foreign policy: An introduction*. New York: Routledge.
Mattern, J. 2007. Why 'soft power' isn't so soft: Representational force and attraction in world politics. In *Power in world politics*, eds. F. Berenskoetter and M. Williams, 583 612. London and New York: Routledge.
McGiffert, C. 2009. *Chinese soft power and its implication for the United States. Competition and cooperation in the developing world*. Washington DC: CSIS.
Mingjiang Li. 2009. Soft power in Chinese discourse: Popularity and prospect. In *Soft power: China's emerging strategy in international politics*, ed. Li Mingjiang, 21–44. Plymouth: Lexington Books.
Nye, J. 1990. Soft power. *Foreign Policy* 80: 153–71.
Nye, J. 2007. Notes for a soft power research agenda. In *Power in world politics*, eds. F. Berenskoetter and M. Williams, 162–72. London and New York: Routledge.
Nye, J. 2009. Get smart: Combining hard and soft power. *Foreign Affairs* 88, no. 4: 160–3.
Patey, L. 2007. State rules: Oil companies and armed conflict in Sudan. *Third World Quarterly* 28, no. 3: 997–1016.
Pelnēns, G., ed. 2010. *The 'humanitarian dimension' of Russian foreign policy toward Georgia, Moldova, Ukraine, and the Baltic States*. Riga: CEEPS.
Pew Global Attitudes Project. 2007. *Pew global attitudes project*. http://pewglobal.org/reports/pdf/256.pdf
Taylor, I. 2006. *China and Africa: Engagement and compromise*. London and New York: Routledge.
Taylor, I. 2009. *China's new role in Africa*. Boulder: Lynn Rienner.
Xiaogang Deng and Lening Zhang 2009. China's cultural exports and its growing cultural power in the world. In *Soft power: China's emerging strategy in international politics*, ed. Mingjiang Li, 143–62. Plymouth: Lexington Books.
Yongjin Zhang. 2009. The discourse of China's soft power and its discontents. In *China's emerging strategy in international politics*, ed. Li Mingjiang, 45–60. Plymouth: Lexington Books.
Zhongying Pang. 2008. China's soft power dilemma: The Beijing consensus revisited. In *Soft power: China's emerging strategy in international politics* ed. Mingjiang Li, 125–42. Plymouth: Lexington Books.

Index

Africa: domestic conflicts 24
African Humanism 55
African leaders: view of China 1
African Peer Review Mechanism (APRM) 78–9
African Studies growth 8
African Union (AU) 78
Africa's resources: conflict 27–37; scramble 29
Aiyar, M. 67
Angola: Chinese financing in 43; investments 49; Luanda 47–8; problems with investments and exports 49; trading with China 42
Angolan credit extensions 48
Angolan Government: management of oil sector 49
Angolan Ministry of Finance 43–4

Baehr, P. 21
Bahgat, G. 32
Banco Nacional de Desenvolvimento Económico e Social 47
Beijing: attitude toward the UN 13; bureaucracy 31; long-term foreign plans 5; relationship with Darfur 18; reputation 20; sovereignty flexibility 23
Beijing Consensus 37, 102
Beijing Review 16
The Brahmi Report 11–12

Carbone, M. 7, 75–89
Chen, Yuan 44
Cheng, J. and Huangao, S. 34
Chengyuan, G. 84
Chiluba, F. 56
China: African Policy 33; factors for interest in Africa 79; foreign policy 66; future relationships 66; improving image 22; investments in Latin America 31; role in international development 83; supporting allies 20; trading with Angola 42
China Daily 13
China Development Bank 44

China Exim Bank: lending policy 45; loan agreements 43; oil 47
China International Fund Ltd 44
China National Petroleum Corporation 32
China Non-ferrous Metal and Mining Company 57
China-Africa Business Council 99
China-Africa Development Fund 79
China-DAC Study Group 88
China's Africa Policy (White Paper) 100
Chinese and African relationship growth 2
Chinese aid to Africa 102
Chinese ambivalence and evolution 19
Chinese companies: in Africa 98; African relationship 3
Chinese exports to USA 3
Chinese Ministry of Foreign Affairs 45
Chinese populations: different countries 100
Collier, P. and Hoeffler, A. 29
Commission for Africa 80
Common Foreign and Security Policy (CFSP) 78
Communist Party of China 10
conflict analysis 28
conflict (contemporary) research 29
Congo 45
copper-mining: Peruvian 31
Corkin, L. 41–50
Cotonou Agreement 77

Da Cruz, V. 41
Darfur Conflict 13, 18, 36
Davies, M. 45
Democratic Republic of Congo 45
Department of Foreign Aid 98
Department of West Asian and African Affairs 98
Desphande, G.: and Gupta, H. 42
Directorate General for Development 81
Disarmament, Demobilisation, and Reintegration (DDR) programme (1999) 17
Downs, E. 32

INDEX

economic arrangements: political context 4
Economic and Commercial Counsellor (ECC) 98
economic comparisons 3
economic development 96
economic development model 2
Economic Partnership Agreements (EPAs) 82
The Economist 31
Ethiopian-Eritrean border war 13
EU and China's rise in Africa 75–89; trilateral cooperation 7, 76
EU Strategy for Africa 76
EU-Africa Infrastructure Partnership 82
Euro-Mediterranean Partnership 77
European Commission 80; proposal 86
European Consensus on Development 76, 78
European Neighbourhood Policy 77
European Parliament 78
European Security and Defense Policy 78

Fijalkowski, L. 7, 95–103
Five Point Proposal 101
Five Principles of Peaceful Coexistence 4, 60
Foot, R. 23
Forum on China-Africa Cooperation 79
Fournier, J.-B. 29
Fraser, A. 53

Gabinete de Reconstrução Nacional (GRN): purpose 44
Gill, B. and Reilly, J. 97–8
Global democratisation - camouflage of US hegemony (Wang) 20
Government Initiative 82
Guangya, W. 9
The Guardian 27
Guijin, L. 84
Gulf War (first) 15
Guofang, S. 21
Gupta, H.: and Desphande, G. 42

Hairong, Y. and Sautman, B. 59
Hanson, S. 35
He, Yin 12
hegemonism 20
Heiligendamm Process 88
hexie shijie: Hu's concept 23
Hoeffler, A.: and Collier, P. 29
honey pot analysis 28, 30; conceptual objections 31
Hu, Jintao, 18, 23, 65, 95; *hexie shijie* 23
Huangao, S.: and Cheng, J. 34

IGO statism 29
independent foreign policy of peace 13
India: entrepreneurship 70; oil demand predictions 66

Indo-American alliance 69
Industrial and Commercial Bank of China 44
International Poverty Reduction Centre 88

Jiang, Zemin 95, 101
Joint Africa-EU Strategy 76–7

Kahl, C.H. 29
Kang, D. 35
Kaunda 55
Keenan, P. 35
Kopiński, D.: and Polus, A. 6–7, 53–62; Polus, A. and Taylor, I. 1–8
Korean War: China's attitude towards UN 6
Kosovo War 17

Le Billon, P. 29
Lee, H.: and Shalmon, D. 46
Li, Baodong, 54, 60–1
Li, Zhaoxing 16
Ling, B 14
Lusaka Ceasefire Agreement (1999) 18

Malacca Straits 69
Mao, Zedong 10, 13, 34, 56
Marton, P. 27–37; and Matura, T. 6
Marxism 30
Mattern, J. 96
Matura, T. 27–37; and Marton, P. 6
Mbeki, T. 61
Meredith, M. 55
Michel, L. 84, 88
Millennium Development Goals (MDGs) 78
Ministry of Commerce 98
Ministry of Foreign Affairs 98
Mogadishu 16
Movimento Popular para Libertação de Angola 41
Mugabe, R. 77
Mukherjee, P. 71
Multi-Facility Economic Zone 60
Multi-Fibre Agreement 3
Mwanawasa, L. 59

Naidu, S.: and Davies, M. 4
Namibia general election (1989) 14
New Partnership for Africa's Development 78
Nigerian National Petroleum Corporation 68
Non-Ferrous Metals Corporation Africa (NFCA) 57
Nye, J. 96–7

oil fields: Rumailah 37; Sakhalin 70
oil sector 65; Angolan Government management 49; Chinese economic activity 2; Chinese oil companies 49; Western oil companies case study 36

INDEX

Pang, Zhongying 10, 102
Patey, L.A. 36
Patriotic Front (PF): Zambia 59
peace conferences: breakthrough 84
peace operations 12–19
peace-support operations 18
peacekeeping operations 19; attitudes 22; growth in Africa 9; in Liberia 20
Peruvian copper-mining 31
Petroleum Engineering Construction Group 99
Pew Global Attitudes Project (2007) 102
Polus, A.: and Kopiński, D. 6–7, 53–62; Kopiński, D. and Taylor, I. 1–8
power: definition 96

Qian, Qichen 12

Reilly, J.: and Gill, B. 97–8
Reno, W.: *Warlord politics and African states* 27
resource curse hypothesis 28
resource security 4
Rumailah oil fields 37

safety conditions: Chinese-owned industries 61
Saich, T. 21
Sakhalin oil fields 70
Sata, M. 54, 59, 61
Sautman, B.: and Hairong, Y. 59
Savimbi, J. 42
Shalmon, D.: and Lee, H. 46
Singh, M. 66, 68, 70
Sino-African relations: aid programmes 33; benefits 3; Chinese discourses 33; energy issues Angola 6; energy issues Zambia 6; similar opinions and common interests 5; weaknesses 3
Sino-Angolan characteristics 48
Sino-Angolan relationship 35, 41–50; evolution 46; progression 50; sustainability 50
Sino-Indian relationship 7, 65–72; benefits 69; bidding wars 68; challenges 67; competition for oil fields 67; consolidation 66; effect on other countries 71; impact on USA 69; lack of technological capability 68; political limits 71
Sino-Pakistan relationship 71
Sino-Western conflict 28
Sino-Zambian relations 7, 53–62; all-weather friendship 56; anti-Chinese demonstrations 60; construction sector 58; increase in interest 61; infrastructure 58; investment 57; mining 56; six features 62
Sinopec 46

Smith, I. 56
Snow, P. 41
soft power: concept origin 95–6; definition 96; incorporation difficulties 97
soft power in Africa 7–8, 95–103; communication 100; difficulties 101; instruments 100
Solana, J. 78
state sovereignty 10–12
State-owned Assets Supervision and Administration Commission (SASAC) 98, 99
strategic partnership: evaluation 48
Sub-Saharan Africa: investment and trade promotion 99
sustainable development 28

Tanzania-Zambia railway (TAZARA) 56
Taylor, I. 41–2, 55; Polus, A. and Kopiński, D. 1–8; and Wu, Zhengyu 5–6
Thompson, D. 14
Tiananmen Square 15, 101
The Times: 'The new scramble for Africa begins' 27
Trade and Development Cooperation Agreement 77
trilateral cooperation 86; Africa's attitude 87–8; China's attitude 87
Tull, D 3

UN African Mission in Darfur (UNAMID) 18
UN Assistance Mission for Rwanda (UNAMIR) 16
UN Department of Peacekeeping Operations (DPKO) 16
UN Mission in the Central African Republic (MINURCA) 17
UN Mission in Sierra Leone (UNAMSIL) 17
UN Mission in Sudan (UNMIS) 18
UN Observer Mission in Angola (MONUA) 17
UN Operation in Mozambique 1994 (ONUMOZ) 15
UN Operation Restore Democracy 15
UN Operation in Somalia (UNOSOM) 16
UN Operation Turquoise 15
UN Organisation Mission in the Democratic Republic of Congo (MONUC) 18
UN Preventive Deployment Force (UNPREDEP) 21
UN Protection Force (UNPROFOR) 15
UN Special Committee on Peacekeeping Operations (UNSCPO) 14
UN Transitional Authority in Cambodia (UNTAC) 15

INDEX

UN Truce Supervision Organisation (UNTSO) 14–15
União Nacional para a Independência Total de Angola (UNITA) 41
United Task Force (UNITAF) 16
US Stabilisation Mission in Haiti (MINUSTAH) 21
US-India partnership 69

Vines, A.: *et al* 44, 48

Wade, A. 82, 87–8
Wallensteen, P. 30
Wang, J.: *Global democratisation - camouflage of US hegemony* 20
Wang, Xue Xia 17

Warlord politics and African states (Reno) 27
Wilson, E. 3
Wu, Zhengyu: and Taylor, I. 5–6
Wysoczańska, K. 7, 65–72

Zambia: characteristics 54; government instability 55; Patriotic Front (PF) 59; role of copper 54
Zambian Consolidated Copper Mines (ZCCM) 55
Zambian Government: importance of China 54
Zhougui Mining Group 57
Zong, He 34